Gathered in My Name
Reflections on Matthew's Gospel

Fr. Don J. West

Edited by Joan Seibenick and Angela Pugliano. Cover design by Angela Pugliano.

Copyright © 2016 Don J. West
All rights reserved. The material contained herein is protected by copyright. No part of it may be republished, copied, reproduced, or adapted without the express written consent of the author.

ISBN: 153998866X
ISBN: 978-1539988663

Contents

Preface

Introduction   1

Advent
Be Prepared   5
Make Time for God   8
Joyful Anticipation   10
The Faith of Mary and Joseph   13

Holy Family
The Power of Family   17

Epiphany
Gifts Fit for a King   21

Baptism of the Lord
Beloved Children of God   25

The Presentation of the Lord
Jesus Begins His Journey   29

Lent
Be Led by the Spirit   33
Finding the Voice of Jesus   36
Live the Gospel   38
So That We May See   41
Open Your Heart to the Good News   44

Palm Sunday
Walk With Jesus   47

Easter
He is Risen   51
The Lord's Forgiveness   54
Hearts Burning With Joy   57
The Lord is Our Protector and Defender   60
Our Journey with Jesus   63
Welcome the Advocate   66

The Ascension
Christ's Disciples   69

Pentecost
The Peace of Jesus   73

Trinity Sunday
The Unity of the Trinity   77

The Feast of Corpus Christi
The Greatest Gift   81

Ordinary Time
Jesus within Us   85
Go Fish!   88
Let Your Light Shine   91
People of Action   93
God's Mercy and Compassion   95
Seeking Out the Kingdom   98
Reconnect With God   100
Life-Giving Soil   103
Hearing the Good News   105
Saying Yes to Jesus   108
Excuses and Solutions   111
Out of the Boat   114
We're all God's Children   117
Who is Jesus?   120
Obstacles or Believers   123
The Power of Prayer   126
God's Generosity   129
Which Child Are You?   132
Sharing Our Rich Harvest   135
To Be Chosen   138
What Belongs to God   141
The Greatest Commandment   144
Good and Faithful Servants   147

Solemnity of Saints Peter and Paul
Leaders   151

The Exaltation of the Holy Cross
The Power of the Cross   155

All Souls' Day
Remembering   159

Christ the King
The Least Ones   163

Preface

My name is Fr. Don West and I'm the pastor of St. John the Evangelist Catholic Church in West Chester, Ohio.

This will be the first of three books and the idea did not originate with me. Each week for our parish bulletin I write a gospel reflection, and I think, in my heart, I wanted to put these thoughts into a book but never thought I could. A parishioner, Leslie N., came to me and said she wanted to put my gospel reflections together in a book. I smiled and said that would be great and left it at that. Later, my friend and co-worker, Joan S., told me Leslie was moving forward with the project. Because of their vision and belief in what I have shared over the years in the bulletin, my gospel reflections are now coming to you in book form. I am grateful for Leslie and Joan's belief in me and the value of the material we present to you.

Introduction

When I was a student in the seminary, a wonderful priest by the name of Fr. Tim Schehr introduced me to the amazing world of the Bible. His passion and heart for scripture was infectious and I couldn't wait to sign up for any course he was teaching. From Fr. Tim I've learned to have some of that same passion and love for scripture and I try to share this with parishioners.

When I write my weekly gospel reflections, I feel blessed to share my thoughts and insights into the Good News that is presented to us each week. I attempt to write about the gospel as if I'm sitting and talking with another person, having a simple, everyday conversation. The conversation isn't too heady and never involves talking down to anyone. It is my hope that these "conversations" will help people consider the possibilities of what Jesus offers to us and to accept the challenge to hear the calling to be Christ for one another.

This book and the next two are organized according to the liturgical years of the church, beginning with the first Sunday of Advent and concluding with the Feast of Christ the King. There are three annual cycles for the Sunday readings affectionately known as Cycles A, B and C. Cycle A focuses on the gospel of

Matthew while Cycle B primarily focuses on the gospel of Mark with several weeks from the gospel of John. The third cycle, C, focuses on the gospel of Luke.

This book focuses on Matthew's gospel, Cycle A readings. It is my hope that, maybe in some way, this journey into Matthew's words will show you how much God loves you and cares for you. I also hope that these reflections might challenge you to fall in love with sacred scripture and see just how wonderful the Good News is.

For where two or three gather in my name, there am I with them.

Matthew 18:20

ADVENT

Be Prepared

> "...stay awake! For you do not know on which day your Lord will come. Be sure of this: if the master of the house had known the hour of the night when the thief was coming, he would have stayed awake and not let his house be broken into. So too, you also must be prepared, for at an hour you do not expect, the Son of Man will come."

Here we begin the season of Advent with a warning. Jesus challenges us to be prepared — to be ready for the coming of the Son of Man.

Advent is always a time of preparing, but sometimes the preparation is more about the material side of Christmas and not the spiritual side. We can be so involved with the decorations and with picking out the right tree for the home that we lose sight of what Christmas is all about. We bake hundreds of cookies, make the pies, and plan our dinner. We attend what seems to be one party after another for work and with our friends. Meanwhile all the stores want you to forget Christmas and have a "Happy Holiday" rather than a Merry Christmas. Just what are we preparing for?

Jesus is telling us that the coming we should be concerned about is the one at the end of our lives. We are told clearly that we won't know when that will take place. What kind of life have we lived in the eyes of the Lord? Jesus tells us to stay awake and be ready. The only way that we can be ready is to remain faithful to the Gospel. We are called to love one another. It really is that simple.

To stay prepared we need to evaluate our lives. There are a number of opportunities during the season of Advent. Perhaps we might need to receive the sacrament of Reconciliation. Perhaps the season calls us to be better at our prayer life. How many of you have an Advent Wreath in your home? How many of you plan on using it during the season? Perhaps you can find an Advent table prayer for the four weeks of Advent. This is a wonderful way to pray with your family as you light the candles on your Advent Wreath.

While Advent is indeed a time to prepare for the baby Jesus to come to us in the manger, it is so much more than that. We are preparing for Jesus to return to the world once more. It is easy to prepare for the material things of Christmas, but it becomes a real challenge to also prepare for Jesus to come again. How are we spiritually preparing for that moment in life? Remaining faith-filled and allowing God's unconditional love to fill our lives make the preparation easier to maintain. As we begin this season of Advent let us remember what the season is all about. Having Jesus at the center is a great way to begin.

Make Time for God

"Repent, for the kingdom of heaven is at hand!"

As we enter the second week of Advent, John the Baptist is challenging people to repent so that they may be found worthy in the kingdom at hand. He calls them to the water to be baptized, for repentance. But John also speaks of another baptism from one mightier than he ~~is:~~ "He will baptize you with the Holy Spirit and fire." And as John's message unfolds, there is a choice to be made. The one who is to come will bring a judgment to all. John describes, "His winnowing fan is in his hand. He will clear his threshing floor and gather his wheat into his barn, but the chaff he will burn with unquenchable fire."

John is setting the table for Jesus to enter into the world. His message echoes the thoughts of week one of Advent: Be prepared! John calls for a change of heart—to turn away from sin, to repent, and to be washed clean. When we have come to the waters of repentance, we are now prepared for the baptism of the Holy Spirit and fire. Once again we are reminded that Advent is more than a time to prepare for the baby Jesus coming into the world. Advent is also a time to prepare for the Lord Jesus to come into our hearts. Are we able to make room for him in our lives? Can we humbly come before the Lord and allow him to baptize us? If we have accepted the baptism, do we allow it flow into our hearts and into our daily lives? This requires more than just lip service. The baptism of Jesus calls us to a change of heart. That is why John preached a baptism of repentance, so that we might be open to receive Jesus into our lives.

The season of Advent is a time for reflection. When we find time to reflect on our lives, we begin to see just how we have accepted the two baptisms. Maybe our lives are so filled with "stuff" of the world that we can't clearly see where God is in our life. Maybe all the trappings of the world have caused us to block out God's redeeming love. Now is the time to come to the waters of repentance. When we take the time to slow down and take stock of our lives, we can see just how little or how much God is in our life. If he isn't at the center of our lives what is holding us back? Making room for God is necessary for our salvation. We always seem to find time for other things in our life; now is the Lord's time. Open your hearts up to the Lord and allow him to fill your lives with hope and with his unconditional love.

Joyful Anticipation

> "Are you the one who is to come, or should we look for another?" Jesus said in reply, "Go and tell John what you hear and see: the blind regain their sight, the lame walk, lepers are cleansed, the deaf hear, the dead are raised, and the poor have the good news proclaimed to them. And blessed is the one who takes no offense at me."

This passage is read for the third Sunday of Advent, and we light the rose candle. It is a Sunday of joyful anticipation. The Gospel reflects that joy. John, the prophet laying down the foundation for Jesus to enter the world, is now in prison. He wants to know if Jesus is the one, the Christ, or if his disciples look for another. It is clear that Jesus is indeed the Messiah. John's work is complete. John will soon lose his life, but as Jesus points out, John was a messenger who prepared the way of the Lord and did his work well. John was more than a prophet. He was someone given the awesome responsibility of making straight the way of the Lord.

Where are we in our preparation? Have you increased your prayers? Did your family get an Advent wreath? I am sure that the preparation for your family has increased greatly. Did you find time for the sacrament of Reconciliation? Is Jesus part of your planning for the season of Christmas? It is not too late to make adjustments in your busy schedule. It will really make a difference in the Christmas season if you have done your preparation correctly. There is nothing wrong with working on the decorations around the house— of course tradition has it that there is no baby Jesus in the crib until Christmas morning. ☺

It may not seem like we have a lot of time until Christmas, but we can put what we do have to good use. Yes, you could spend time baking and shopping but don't forget to have quality time for God. In Matthew's Gospel, Jesus shows us that he is the Messiah who restores life and order in the kingdom. Jesus brings a healing sense into our injured world. He reaches out to the outcasts, those people that seem to remain on the fringe of life. We have the opportunity to reach out to others just as Jesus did

We are called to build up the kingdom, but we really can't do that if we need healing. We must seek out the Lord and humbly ask him to make us whole. When we experience the healing nature of our loving savior, then we can reach out to others. Let us not lose sight of what this season is all about. It is a time for preparation but it also a time for joyful anticipation. Jesus calls us into the kingdom of God. He wants to make us whole, and we are humbly called to bring others this Good News.

The Faith of Mary and Joseph

> "Joseph, son of David, do not be afraid to take Mary your wife into your home. For it is through the Holy Spirit that this child has been conceived in her. She will bear a son and you are to name him Jesus, because he will save his people from their sins."

We have reached the Fourth Sunday of Advent with this Gospel. In just a few days we will be celebrating Christmas, but on this fourth Sunday of Advent we get to view the unfolding through the eyes of Joseph.

While it is unanimously agreed that Mary had tremendous faith to believe what the angel told her, I believe Joseph had that same faith. Mary knew that the Holy Spirit brought her the gift of life. Now it was Joseph's time to have faith in the angel. This was no ordinary child—Jesus was coming into the world to save his people from their sins. The prophets foretold it; his name shall be Emmanuel, which means, "God is with us." Joseph's faith allowed him to welcome his wife into his home with a child to soon be born. Mary and Joseph had such deep faith. They were blessed with a special gift: Jesus the Son of God. He is the one who came into the world to bring salvation to all.

So is there still time to make room for Jesus in our busy lives? For some, I am sure it seems difficult to make time for Jesus. Could you imagine if Mary or Joseph didn't have time for Jesus? What if they were too busy to make room for the Savior of the world? They humbly said *yes* even though they didn't know the end of the story as we do. Their faith allowed their lives to be changed in ways they could never have imagined. It is easy to get caught up in the last minute preparation for Christmas—making sure all the presents are bought, the last minute baking is finished, and the house cleaning is done for family and friends who will soon visit. Perhaps we take time to replace the burned out lights on the tree or, for some, maybe there's some time spent in recalling where we put the baby Jesus for the crib in the nativity scene.

No matter how busy you are in the next couple of days, take time to clear a little space in your heart for Jesus. Jesus, after all, is the reason for the season. We are preparing for Jesus to once again come into our life in a special way. The spirit that this season brings can give us such a wonderful feeling. Take some quiet time away from all the "stuff" that needs to be done and spend it in prayer. I personally love to spend some quiet time in front of the nativity scene. It brings back so many wonderful memories. It reminds me of the simple way that Jesus broke through human history. When this Gospel is read at church, Christmas is quickly coming upon us. Please remember how much Jesus loves you and wants to be a part of your life.

HOLY FAMILY

The Power of Family

> "…the angel of the Lord appeared to Joseph in a dream and said, 'Rise, take the child and his mother, flee to Egypt, and stay there until I tell you. Herod is going to search for the child to destroy him.'"

This Gospel marks the celebration of the feast of The Holy Family of Jesus, Mary, and Joseph. Matthew tells of the trouble that surrounds Jesus and his family shortly after Jesus' birth. Herod wants to destroy "the newborn king." Joseph listens to the angel and takes Jesus and Mary into Egypt. In fear for their lives, he led them to safety. Just like Joseph, parents would take any step necessary to protect their family. The family is a sacred thing, and people will do whatever it takes to keep them safe. Joseph is a model for all of us—his faith and trust in his dream saved Jesus and Mary's life.

On the Feast of the Holy Family, we are called to reflect on our own family. My family is a lot smaller than when I was growing up. Over the years many of my family members have passed, but the family I have—my sister and her husband, along with my nieces and nephews and great nephews—is simply awesome. I am so lucky to have a loving family. While I don't get to see them as much as I would like, it just makes the time I do have with them more memorable. The Christmas season is about family. When we look at the Holy Family we see God's handiwork at its best. Just as our heavenly Father watched out for Jesus, Mary, and Joseph, He also looks out for us. He gives us grace that guides us from danger into His unconditional love. We may never have the challenges that faced the Holy Family, but God's love for us is just as strong.

We may not learn from our dreams as Joseph did, but God still communicates with us. Through our prayer life we continue to keep open the lines of communication. In our conversations with God we learn what is needed to guide and protect us. We are God's family. Be sure to celebrate your family. If your family is strained or hurting, lift them up to the Father. Let God's healing love bring peace to your family. God has brought us to the earth to celebrate life—let us rejoice! I am grateful for my family—not only my biological family but also my church family. It is a blessing for me to be a part of my parish family. While we may not be perfect in all things, we are indeed Christ-centered.

EPIPHANY

Gifts Fit for a King

> "They were overjoyed at seeing the star, and on entering the house they saw the child with Mary his mother. They prostrated themselves and did him homage. Then they opened their treasures and offered him gifts of gold, frankincense, and myrrh."

We celebrate the Epiphany of the Lord with this passage. Sometimes this feast is called the "Little Christmas." When I worked at a home for children in Michigan, we always had a big celebration on January 6th. The children would all come back to the home after being with what family they had. These children were wards of the court—truly sad cases. Many generous donors would step up each year and make sure these children had a great Christmas. It was heartwarming to see the joy in their eyes.

The Magi may have had the same look in their eyes as they gazed upon the face of Jesus for the first time. They may have been breathless as they looked at the newborn king. The magi paid Jesus homage and offered him their gifts—gifts fit for a king. The Magi had been following a star that led them to Jesus. Now Jesus is our light. The light shines brightly for us to follow, but there are times when that light isn't seen as clearly as we would like to see it. We may also have to stop and get directions to help us focus once again on the light given to us.

When we come before the Lord, what gift will we lay before his feet? Do we have gifts fit for a king? I am sure you have received many wonderful gifts this Christmas season; perhaps there are a few that will remain in the closet. What is it that we can give the Lord? Do we simply give something out of our reserve or something stuck in our closet and not our best? When we are too busy, that is what we often do: give from our reserve, if we give at all. Jesus gives us the very best: His life. Are we grateful for what the Lord has given us? When we come to the Eucharistic table, do we know what a powerful gift we are about to receive? Do we take time to thank Jesus for his life?

The season of Christmas is coming to an end. Our gift-giving doesn't have to end with Christmas. We are all called to be grateful for what we have. It may be short of what we think we should have, but with Jesus dwelling in our hearts we can't go wrong. As this New Year begins, let us all work on sharing our gifts. May we come before the Lord and give him our best. Let us make an effort to let the Lord know how grateful we are. Each of us has been blessed with many gifts, talents, and treasures; let us share them for the good of the kingdom.

BAPTISM OF THE LORD

Beloved Children of God

"After Jesus was baptized, he came up from the water and behold, the heavens were opened for him, and he saw the Spirit of God descending like a dove and coming upon him. And a voice came from the heavens, saying, 'This is my beloved Son with whom I am well pleased.'"

We read this Gospel as we celebrate the Baptism of the Lord. John the Baptist was confused because he felt that Jesus should baptize him, but that was not meant to be. Jesus was embracing his humanness—setting an example for the people. Jesus had no need for repentance, but as Jesus spoke to John, "Allow it now, for thus it is fitting for us to fulfill all righteousness." John couldn't refuse such a request.

Jesus knew this moment was the beginning of his public ministry. The heavens opened and the Spirit was upon him. Jesus heard his Father affirm His Son. The Father was well pleased with His Son and that he was being sent forth from the waters of the Jordan out into the world. It would be awesome to see the heavens open and then hear the Father say, "This is my beloved son/daughter with whom I am well pleased." Then we would know for sure that we are heading in the right direction. Some people hear the

Father's words more clearly than others. That doesn't mean we are not his beloved. God loves us and wants the best for us.

The best might be coming to the waters of John's Baptism, letting go of our sins, and repenting. When we have cleared away everything that prevents a right relationship with the Lord, we can feel as though a burden has been lifted off of our shoulders. Jesus came to the Jordan that day to begin his earthly ministry. He, by his actions, confirmed the message that John had been giving the people.

Now it is time to move on and open up fully to the message that Jesus has to offer each of us. Are we spiritually prepared for that encounter? We are ready as long as we open our hearts to the grace that Jesus has to give us. He reaches out and takes us by the hand and leads us down the path of salvation. It begins with that simple gesture of Baptism. When we were baptized, we were baptized into Jesus' life, death, and resurrection. We were made a part of God's family. We are God's beloved sons and daughters, and we are brothers and sisters of Jesus. Jesus came down to earth so that we may have life, a life that is full of God's compassion and love. We must always be open to unloading anything that keeps us from a solid relationship with God. We must continue to be his beloved. Knowing that the Father's love is all around us gives a sense of security. Let us embrace the goodness of our savior and feel the warmth of his love.

THE PRESENTATION OF THE LORD

Jesus Begins His Journey

> "Simeon blessed them and said to Mary his mother, 'Behold this child is destined for the fall and rise of many in Israel, and to be a sign that will be contradicted—and you yourself a sword will pierce—so that the thoughts of many hearts may be revealed.'"

The feast of the Presentation of the Lord is celebrated 40 days after Christmas. It was a time when Joseph and Mary came to the temple to present Jesus. They were to sacrifice two turtledoves or pigeons to the Lord. During this feast, the church has a ritual of blessing all the candles that will be used during the church year. The only exception is the Easter Candle which is prepared, blessed, and lit during the Easter Vigil.

Can you imagine what must have been going through Mary's mind as Simeon spoke to her? The whole world was being opened up to Jesus and then Simeon told of the life that was set before Jesus. It doesn't sound like a smooth ride, but Simeon was right: God indeed had shown the journey of Jesus.

I can only imagine the joy that parents have as they present their children to the church today for Baptism. As the parents and godparents stand with the child in their arms, what hopes and dreams must go through their minds? They know that the journey of this little boy or girl will not always be easy, but they will support the child. It is their responsibility to introduce them into the faith they were baptized into; something all parents need to ponder from time to time.

Simeon's words are challenging as well. He speaks of the good that Jesus will bring to the world. Since there is free will, each person will have to choose whether to accept or reject the words of Jesus. Mary's life will be pierced as she sees her son grow up and begin his mission on earth. Mary will feel the pain and suffering that her son will endure for the salvation of all. Her *yes* to God will be a gift to the world, but it is a gift that all will not accept. It is a gift that people will literally try to destroy.

On this Feast of the Presentation of the Lord, what do we present before the Lord? Is our faith as strong as it can be? Have we accepted the gift of Jesus into our hearts? Have we taken the gift of Jesus and made him a daily part of life? Do we share that gift with others? Perhaps it is time to re-commit ourselves to the Lord. It is time to open our hearts to the love of the Lord. He so wants to be a part of our lives. He knows that this life presents challenges to all of us, but he remains with us always. As Jesus took his journey to the cross for our sins, his mother went with him to love and support him. We all need support in our life journey. May we always feel the supportive presence of Jesus in our lives.

LENT

Be Led by the Spirit

"At the time Jesus was led by the Spirit into the desert to be tempted by the devil. He fasted for forty days and forty nights, and afterwards he was hungry."

On the first Sunday of Lent, we begin the journey through the desert. Are we being led by the Spirit? The devil will be along on our journey to tempt us, trying to lead us away from a right relationship with the Lord. Satan is so good at what he does. As we see in today's Gospel, he tried to work his influence on Jesus with the three temptations. Finally Jesus sent him away saying, "Get away, Satan!" Satan is no match for a spirit-filled Jesus.

So the journey begins. What plans do you have for the season of Lent? Is there a spiritual nature to your journey? Are you making any sacrifices during this season of Lent? How are you preparing for the joys of Easter? How are we going to grow spiritually this Lent?

I try to do something spiritually enriching during Lent, like read something that will help me grow deeper in my relationship with God. There are many daily scripture readings to read during Lent. I also try to give up something during Lent. It's usually something I enjoy eating or drinking to remind me of what Jesus sacrificed for us.

For some of us, Lenten sacrifices are about as successful as New Years' resolutions. They start out strong, but after the first week or so they seem to slip from our memories. We have to work a little harder to keep them alive for the entire season of Lent.

When we enter the desert with the Spirit, he can guide us when we start to drift. We have to remain strong and trust as Jesus did. When Satan offers us something tempting, ask yourself, "Where is God in this situation?" Will this offering lead me to an authentic relationship with Jesus? As we hear in today's Gospel, giving into temptation sounds good, but Jesus knew that the devil really has nothing good to offer at all. Satan's goal is to destroy God's love in us. Sooner or later, we have to say to the devil, "Get away Satan." Three simple words that we must always have handy, for the devil will never give up. The good news is that God's love is stronger and more rewarding than anything that Satan can offer us.

This Lent, let us focus on our relationship with the Lord. How can we make this relationship deeper? Lent is a time for penance—a time for spiritual house cleaning. Take time to make room for God in your life. Pray more, do for others, renew yourself spiritually. Your reward will be great. Easter will bring a true resurrection for you.

Finding the Voice of Jesus

"While he was still speaking, behold, a bright cloud cast a shadow over them, then from the cloud came a voice that said, 'This is my beloved Son, with whom I am well pleased, listen to him.'"

At this sight and sound, Peter, James, and John must have felt overwhelmed. Here they were on a mountain top with Jesus, Moses, and Elijah. No wonder Peter wanted to put up three tents so they could hold on to the experience! An experience like this would change a person forever. The cloud and the voice bring the scene back to focus on God's son. Jesus is the fulfillment of the law, Moses, and the prophet, Elijah. Salvation is all about Jesus and his mission on earth. That is why Jesus could not let Peter build the tents and why Jesus told the three apostles, "Do not tell the vision to anyone until the Son of Man has been raised from the dead." In any case, who would believe them without some kind of proof? Jesus knew staying on the mountain was not part of the plan.

The voice from the cloud calls us to listen to Jesus. That means more than hearing the words, it means acknowledging and understanding. When our lives are open to the words of Jesus, then we too can be on the right path. Sometimes in our lives we have far too many voices talking to us, and it is hard to listen to the Lord. Many of the voices will lead us away from Jesus. The voices at first sound wonderful and we fall victim to sin. Suddenly we are far away from Christ, let alone near any mountain top experience. We need to transform our lives once again, focusing on the Lord. How do we do that? Well, we have to find the voice of Jesus. God has given us his son so that we might continue to be in a right relationship with Him. Once we hear Jesus' voice and renew our acceptance of the Gospel, we can continue to be a part of the kingdom.

Sometimes when the voices lead us astray, they lead us to sin. Sin puts up barriers and we become lost. When sin overwhelms us, we need to reconcile with the Lord. The season of Lent gives many opportunities for the Sacrament of Reconciliation. If you haven't experienced Reconciliation in a while, make plans to do so. Set yourself free and embrace God's forgiveness, then we will be God's beloved children.

Live the Gospel

> "We no longer believe in him because of your word; for we have heard for ourselves, and we know that this is truly the savior of the world."

The woman at the well—like Peter, James, and John in the previous Gospel—must have felt overwhelmed by Jesus' presence. She is never named, and I have often wondered why not. The disciples seem confused, as always, about what Jesus offered to the woman and to the people of the Samaritan town. In two days, Jesus moved a town from tolerating the woman's story to realizing that the savior is alive and well and walking among them.

At some time in our life, we all have to reach the realization of the townspeople. We may hear others' stories, but until we make it our own, it stays a story, not a revelation. Make the Gospel your own. Allow Jesus to change your heart, and open up to the revelation that Jesus is our Lord and Savior. Then we will find ourselves in communion with the whole Body of Christ. When Jesus' message becomes clear in our minds and in our hearts, when we begin to live the Gospel, it becomes a way of life. It is no longer something we hear at Mass—it is who we are. What a rush it is to know that we are saved—that Jesus has called us unto himself. Although we are sinners, Jesus wants to heal us and make us whole. Notice in today's Gospel that Jesus never calls the woman a sinner. He doesn't dwell on her past. What is important to Jesus is bringing salvation to her. He wants to give her living water so that she never thirsts again. It is the same water that Jesus wants to give to us.

The people of the town knew the woman well. Perhaps they had even passed judgment on her. Yet when she came with the news of the Messiah, they began to open up to the possibility that the woman might be right. They came and invited Jesus to come to their town. It was an invitation they would never regret. We too have to invite Jesus into our lives. We have to open our hearts so that he may find a place to dwell. Ask the Lord to come to you. He waits for our invitation. The story we may have heard from others now becomes our story. We believe Jesus is our savior because now we have felt him in our own lives. Do more than hear the stories about others' experiences of Jesus. Have your own story to tell. If we have forgotten part of the story, it is never too late to turn to Jesus and connect with him again. As we begin to live out our story, we share it with others. Be a light for others. The woman at the well can teach us many wonderful things, but the most amazing thing is that Jesus is the savior of the world.

So That We May See

> "'Do you believe in the Son of Man?' He answered
> and said, 'Who is he, sir, that I may believe in him?'
> Jesus said to him, 'You have seen him, and the one
> speaking with you is he.' He said, 'I do believe, Lord,'
> and he worshipped him."

On the fourth Sunday of Lent we once again hear the powerful story of the man born blind, a story of conversion. The blind man had faith in Jesus from the moment the two met. The blind man's journey led him to a confrontation with the Jewish officials who tried to deny the Christ. The Gospel tells how the Pharisees were so set to discredit Jesus. Through it all, the blind man stuck with the facts and was primed for Jesus calling him to be his disciple.

That moment when Jesus came to the blind man and asked him if he believed in the Son of Man would forever change the blind man's life. It is interesting that once again the person Jesus heals is nameless. As the woman at the well is unnamed, so too the blind man is unnamed, and this calls us to see ourselves in these two people. Our lives may be different from the woman at the well, but we all have barriers keeping us from a right relationship with the Lord. We might be able to see in the literal sense, but all of us have been blind to the love of God.

The story of the blind man shows Jesus' compassion. Jesus makes clay and puts it on the man's eyes. The man feels the healing sensation as he goes to the pool to wash away his blindness. When you think about it, others in the reading remained blind. The parents wanted to avoid being sent from the synagogue, the apostles were concerned whose sin it was, and the Pharisees painted Jesus as a sinner.

We all want to avoid the blindness of the parents, apostles, and Pharisees. We ask Jesus to take away the obstructions that blind us from believing in Jesus as the Son of Man. When we do finally come face to face with our Lord and Savior, we will celebrate our sight being restored. We have to come to him and humbly ask him for our sight. He will touch our hearts and give us the grace to see him clearly in our lives. With our eye sight restored, we can look at the world in a different, loving way.

As we continue our journey through Lent, let us work on what is holding us back from loving God and our neighbor. Seek the Lord and ask for his healing touch. Jesus is never far from us—all he waits for is an invitation into our lives. Let us find ourselves like the man born blind: Come before Jesus and say, "I do believe Lord," and worship him. What an awesome God we have! Let us rejoice in his mercy.

Open Your Heart to the Good News

> "Jesus told [Martha], 'I am the resurrection and the life; whoever believes in me, even if he dies, will live, and everyone who lives and believes in me will never die. Do you believe this?' She said, 'Yes, Lord. I have come to believe that you are the Christ, the Son of God, the one who is coming into the world.'"

In the beginning of this Gospel, Martha and Jesus are talking about the death of Lazarus, Martha and Mary's brother. Martha shows that she has a firm grasp of who Jesus is and his mission. She makes a profession of faith before Jesus. Jesus speaks of eternal life—those who believe in him will never die. Martha knows Jesus is the anointed one of God—His only son.

When we profess our belief in Jesus, do we truly believe what we are saying? Does our life back up what we say about who Jesus is and what he means to us? Jesus proclaims that he is the one who will bring salvation to the world. The Father has sent him into the world to bring life to all who believe. We must come to know Jesus and believe in him. Jesus is the source of eternal life. No matter what happens in our life, if we remain faithful, we will never die. Even though our earthly life may pass, there is a life waiting for us that is eternal. Do we believe this? Does our life reflect a true connection with Jesus?

There is more in this Gospel than the raising of Lazarus: those who put their trust into Jesus will see the glory of God as the stone was moved from the tomb. As Jesus called Lazarus from the tomb, the reality of life over death is shown. Jesus told them to untie him and let him go free. What joy must have been in Martha and Mary's hearts! There were many people there to witness the miracle; I wonder how many shared Martha's conviction.

Lent is quickly coming to an end and soon we will enter Holy Week. How has this Lent been for you? Have you kept your Lenten promises? Have those promises made a difference in your spiritual life? Are there things that you need to let go of so you may be able to journey with Jesus to the Last Supper? Are you ready to go to the cross and die with him? Is your life in order to experience the Easter joys? Jesus opens himself up to us. He reveals that he is the Son of God. We need to work to open our hearts to the Good News. Don't let Easter pass you by. Follow Martha's response to Jesus. Jesus is always around, ready to be welcomed into our lives. Our belief in Jesus will give us life eternal. Set yourself free and embrace the living God.

PALM SUNDAY

Walk With Jesus

> "Jesus advanced a little and fell prostrate in prayer, saying, 'My Father, if it is possible, let this cup pass from me, yet, not as I will, but as you will.'"

In this passage read for Palm Sunday we are listening to the Passion of the Lord from Matthew's Gospel. We begin the holy journey with Jesus to the cross.

In the garden, Jesus had a prayer that alluded to the fact that he would allow the cup to pass by him. Three times Jesus came to the Father with the same words, but there was something that showed, as always, that he was truly on this earth to do the will of the Father: "Not as I will, but as you will." Each time he went to pray, he was focused on the will of the Father.

Unfortunately Peter, James, and John were blind to the message Jesus had for them. He asked them to pray as well. He knew their strength would be tested. What did the apostles do? They fell asleep. They could not pray even an hour with Jesus. As Jesus' betrayer approached, Jesus rallied the apostles to wake and face what was about to happen. Judas was before them with an angry crowd coming to arrest Jesus. Jesus knew that he would suffer greatly at the hands of others.

During Holy Week, we are called to come pray with Jesus. We are invited to the Holy Thursday meal and to take the journey to the cross to experience once again what Jesus did for us. Then we celebrate the joy of the resurrection of Jesus. By the size of the crowds on Easter Sunday, many come to celebrate the resurrection; however, there are fewer people joining in the journey to Easter Sunday.

Perhaps we are like the apostles: We know we are invited to pray, but also like the apostles, we fall asleep. We lose interest. It is unfortunate to see a sparse crowd for Holy Thursday. We gather that evening to wash one another's feet and to celebrate the Eucharist, God's wonderful gift of his son to us. Good Friday calls us to walk with Jesus to the cross and remember what Jesus did for each of us. The Easter Vigil is one of the most powerful liturgies and isn't always well attended in some parishes. If you haven't been to an Easter Vigil celebration, you are missing something special. I hope you will make time to experience the Vigil.

Jesus asked us to pray and walk with him this week. Are we up for the journey? Can we make time for Jesus? Does Jesus matter in our life? How do we show it? It is easy to rush to the Easter joys, but we don't experience the full effect of the journey by skipping to

Sunday. We are a family of believers. I invite each of you to let Holy Week make a difference in your spiritual life. This is our salvation; this is our faith. Let us share it with one another.

EASTER

He is Risen

> "...He is not here, for he has been raised just as he said. Come and see the place where he lay. Then go quickly and tell his disciples, 'He has been raised from the dead, and he is going before you to Galilee; there you will see him.'"

On Easter morning, Mary and Mary Magdalene went to the tomb. There had been an earthquake and the stone had rolled away. They encountered an angel who told them that Jesus had risen. They must have felt shock and fear all at the same time, but they also had to believe the good news from the angel. This wasn't any ordinary news; he told them that Jesus was alive and going to Galilee. It must have taken great faith for them to believe in such news. The women had an encounter with Jesus on the way. He spoke to them to calm them down and reinforced the need to tell the apostles what Jesus called them to do. The women become the first evangelists post-resurrection.

They headed to Galilee where there would be a reunion. How would the apostles react to the news? Would they believe the women? How do we take the news of the risen Lord? Our churches are full on Easter Sunday morning. Families unite to celebrate our salvation. Jesus died for our sins. He has opened the gates of heaven for each of us because he loves us deeply. What happens to the joy of Easter after Easter Sunday? The Church takes seven Sundays to celebrate Easter, but in reality we celebrate Easter every time we gather for Mass. Where do all the people go? Why don't we have the same joy every Sunday as we do on Easter morning? Perhaps we get too comfortable with our faith. It's there, but we don't make the effort to nurture it. Maybe we have a little bit of apathy in our faith lives. We have lost interest in the Mass. We feel we can get God on our own terms. We can talk to him any time.

Why do we need a faith community to share what we see as a private relationship? The answer lies in the Easter Gospel: a community of believers gathered because they heard about Jesus' resurrection. The women went in haste to the apostles so they too could join in the celebration. Jesus came to them at Galilee, took away their fears, and gave them new hope. When we look into the empty tomb, what do we see? We see hope. Do we believe in the risen Lord? Our faith is nothing without the realization that not only did Jesus die, but he also rose from the dead. When we accept this, we are forever changed. We are called to share that Good News. We are called to live that

Good News. Let us always be Easter people rejoicing in Jesus and our salvation.

The Lord's Forgiveness

"'…Peace be with you. As the Father has sent me, so I send you.' And when he had said this, he breathed on them and said to them, 'Receive the Holy Spirit. Whose sins you forgive are forgiven them, and whose sins you retain are retained.'"

The disciples were locked in a room full of fear. They were afraid that they would also be arrested and put to death. They did not want the same fate their leader had. So what did Jesus do? He entered the locked room and met their fears. The first thing that the risen Christ offered was peace. He showed them his wounds. He showed that he was really alive.

Jesus came to ease their fears but also to give them a command. He came to send them into the world. As he was sent by the Father, now he sends his disciples. The Good News is at hand, the time is now. Jesus gave them the gift of the Holy Spirit that would keep that peace alive in their heart. The Holy Spirit would give them the courage to go out and face the world.

Jesus' whole life was about showing the Father's love. He met people where they were and healed their brokenness. He came to repair relationships that had been broken through sin. His compassion brought many back to God. It was time for the disciples to do the same. Jesus spoke to his disciples about forgiving sins. For those who had a contrite heart, Jesus told them to offer forgiveness for their sins. For those who did not show contrition, forgiveness should not be given to them. There has to be some acknowledgement of the wrongs that we have committed and we must do this with a sincere heart. Then we can turn and ask for forgiveness.

What fears are holding you back from a right relationship with God? Is there a fear that you can't be forgiven? Is it time to surrender to the power of the Lord's forgiveness? Jesus comes into our lives and wants to make us whole. He is the one who sets us free so that we may be his disciple. Once we allow the Lord into our lives, we are called to lead others to him. He gives us the gift of the Holy Spirit. He places his peace in our hearts. How can we refuse such a gift? Even Thomas believed when Jesus came to him to take away his stubbornness. Jesus revealed his sacred wounds and challenged Thomas to stop his disbelief. Jesus will do the same for each of us. He will break through the walls that we have built and meet us face to face. Will you welcome him into your lives? Are you willing to open your heart to his compassionate love? Once you have received that love and felt his forgiveness, are you willing to do the same for others? What freedom we have when we follow Jesus' lead. Call Jesus into your life and allow him to set you free.

Hearts Burning With Joy

"And it happened that, while he was with them at the table, he took bread, and said the blessing, broke it, and gave it to them. With that their eyes were opened and they recognized him but he vanished from their sight. Then they said to each other, 'Were not our hearts burning within us…'"

This reading from the third Sunday of Easter tells the powerful story of the two disciples on the road to Emmaus. I just love this story. Jesus spoke to the disciples as they walked along the road and, not knowing it was Jesus, they invited him in to have a meal. They knew how to offer hospitality to a stranger, yet they still had to notice something special about this man. He spoke to their hearts and they were alive with the Good News. Jesus broke the bread, blessed it, and shared it with them. They were in communion with the Lord, and at once they came to recognize Jesus. With that, he was gone. Or was he gone? He actually was in their hearts—in the breaking of the bread. Perhaps the words spoken at the Last Supper flashed into their heads: "Take and eat…this is my body…do this in remembrance of me." They once again shared that special moment where they received Jesus. They returned to Jerusalem to share the Good News. There were others who saw the risen Lord, and the disciples were excited because the risen Christ was among them.

What a great Eucharistic meal story. Wouldn't it be awesome if we could get that excited when we gather for the meal? It is Easter and we should rejoice and celebrate. Easter is not a one day event. Every time we gather for the breaking of the bread, we remember what Jesus did for us: He gave his life for our salvation. I wish all of us could feel that burning of our hearts as we receive the Eucharist. Jesus is revealed in the bread and the wine. His body and blood are there for the taking.

One of my deep fears is that few really see the true presence of Jesus in the Eucharist. Our churches should be filled with believers coming to the table of the Lord. We should be grateful for the opportunity to receive Jesus on a regular basis. Our salvation hinges on this wonderful sacrament. It is the foundation of our faith. We need to re-capture the excitement that the early disciples had. We need to let Jesus set our hearts on fire. It is time to allow sacred scripture to open our eyes to the wonderful gift of salvation. And when the story becomes our own and our hearts burn with the joy of the risen Lord, then we can be disciples to others. Through our lives, we can share the excitement and the joy. Invite the Lord into your life. Allow him to re-kindle the fire in your hearts. Open yourself up to the Good News!

The Lord is Our Protector and Defender

> "I am the gate. Whoever enters through me will be saved, and will come in and go out and find pasture. A thief comes only to steal and slaughter and destroy; I came so that they might have life and have it more abundantly."

It seems impossible to read this message from Jesus and not feel his love. Jesus attacked the Pharisees and told them they were poor leaders. They were like thieves who came to steal and slaughter and destroy. They took away the very life that Jesus was trying to offer people. The Pharisees wouldn't allow themselves to see the power of Jesus in their lives. If they couldn't see it for their own lives, how could they ever want it for others?

Jesus' words are meant to bring comfort. When we surrender to the Lord, we can find life is much easier. We don't have to face the challenges alone. Jesus' voice is a voice that calms us and brings a peaceful heart. But in a world filled with so many voices, it can be difficult to hear the Lord calling us. When we aren't careful, strangers may sound enticing and alluring. When we listen too closely to the wrong voices, we can be led away from the Lord and what he has to offer to us. We need to find ways to tune out those voices. We need to focus our hearts on Jesus. Jesus is the source of life that we need to follow. When we enter the "gate" we know that we are home.

Our prayer lives should allow us to tune out those strangers who call out to us. When we encounter people who aren't authentic about showing us the love of God, we need to change the channel. There are many around us that claim that they have heard Jesus call them, but they usually have their own agendas in mind. People who have a one-dimensional view of life lose sight of the Lord's plan for us. They can do more harm than good. Jesus will continue to call us unto himself. He wants us to find the safety of his love. Even though there are many Pharisee-like people in the world, they can't keep us from a loving relationship with Jesus.

Jesus is calling to each of us. We have to listen carefully to that call and enter through Jesus, the gate. When we find a home with Jesus, he will care for us and nourish us. Jesus has given us his Body and Blood so that we might have life to the fullest. When we are nourished by his Body and Blood, we can stand strong against the negative voices that come into our lives. With Jesus as a source of our protection, no thief can steal us away. When we belong to the Lord, no one can destroy us. We are totally his and he will protect us from all harm if we put our trust in him. What a comfort it is to have the Lord as our protector and our defender.

Our Journey with Jesus

"Philip said to him, 'Master, show us the Father, and that will be enough for us.' Jesus said to him, 'Have I been with you for so long a time and you still do not know me Philip? Whoever has seen me has seen the Father. How can you say, "Show us the Father?" Do you not believe that I am in the Father and the Father is in me?'"

Jesus had spent his whole public ministry revealing his Father to the world. As Jesus revealed himself to his disciples he was at the same time showing them the Father's love. In today's Gospel, you can hear the frustration in the dialogue. Jesus thought that his disciples knew him and knew where he was going. From the responses of Thomas and Philip, it is obvious that they were clueless.

Jesus tried to reassure the disciples, "You have faith in God, have faith in me." They needed to put their trust in Jesus and allow him to lead them home. They just didn't seem to understand, and actually, none of this would make sense to them until after Jesus died and the Holy Spirit came into their lives. Then their eyes opened. They finally understood the mission Jesus had that he gave to each of them.

The relationship between Jesus and the Father is profoundly sacred. The Father so loved the world that he sent his son to save it. Jesus even promised that he had prepared a place for us so that when our lives come to an end on earth, we may be with him and the Father forever. Jesus is the only way to the Father. If we follow his lead, we will find peace in our lives.

Sometimes we are like the disciples in this Gospel. We may know a lot about our faith, but there are times we just don't "get it." We make our relationship with God complicated. When we cut out all the distractions and focus on Jesus, life becomes a little more sensible. It's all about our relationship with Jesus. Do we feel his presence in our life? Do we recognize that Jesus is showing us the Father's love? Jesus wants us to have no obstacles in our way for coming to the Father. It is his mission to bring us home. When we finally understand his mission, it is an awesome feeling. That pure love between the Father and the Son is shared with each of us.

We know where Jesus is going and we know the way, but just because we know doesn't mean we can sit back and watch the world go by. We have to actively live the Gospel. It is not enough to know the way; we have to actually make the journey ourselves. Jesus gives us food for the journey in his Body and Blood.

We can look to Jesus for guidance. It is a journey well worth taking.

Welcome the Advocate

> "If you love me, you will keep my commandments. And I will ask the Father, and he will give you another Advocate to be with you always, the Spirit of truth, whom the world cannot accept, because it neither sees nor knows him. But you know him, because he remains with you, and will be in you."

Jesus prepared his disciples for his departure, but he wanted to assure them they would not be left alone. If they kept his commandments, the Father would send the Advocate, the Holy Spirit that would remain in them. Jesus knew he would soon die, rise, and eventually ascend into heaven. But, as Jesus told his disciples, he would not leave them alone.

The Archbishop confirmed a number of our young high school students recently. In the months prior, they met and studied in preparation for that evening. The Archbishop prayed over them to receive the Holy Spirit and then anointed them with Sacred Chrism. It was powerful to be part of the experience. All of us who have been confirmed received the Advocate that Jesus promised; the Holy Spirit is the one that Jesus gave us to defend and protect us in our journey. Jesus says that out of love we should keep the commandments he gave to us. These commandments are simply to love God and our neighbor with our whole being. On paper that sounds easy. Who doesn't love God? Well if we don't love our neighbors, it's difficult to convince God that we love him. We don't just have a "God and me" relationship; God is bigger than that. Jesus demands his disciples to reach out beyond themselves. Once we experience Jesus' love, we must share it. Our relationship with Jesus has a bond that he will never break. He speaks of the union between the Father, Son, and Holy Spirit. The same love that Jesus has for us is a reflection of the love the Father has for us. The Father's love grants us the Spirit to dwell within us and guide us in our journey.

There is a communion among us when the Father, Son, and Holy Spirit are revealed to us and dwell with us. It should give us comfort that we are not alone. Just as Jesus promised the Advocate to his disciples for when he physically left this world, he also gives the Advocate to us. We are called to remain faithful. No matter what comes along in our life, Jesus will be with us. The love he shows us is the love we are called to share with others. Jesus wants us involved in the building of the kingdom. Let us welcome the Advocate into our lives and allow the Spirit to continue to guide us. Jesus will never let us down.

THE ASCENSION

Christ's Disciples

"When Jesus had said this, as they were looking on, he was lifted up, and a cloud took him from their sight. While they were looking intently at the sky as he was going, suddenly two men dressed in white garments stood beside them. They said, 'Men of Galilee, why are you looking at the sky? This Jesus who has been taken up from you into heaven will return in the same way as you have seen him going into heaven.'"

We read this passage when we celebrate the Ascension of the Lord. With his ascension into heaven, Jesus' earthly life came to an end and the work of the apostles began. Jesus told his followers to return to Jerusalem to wait for the coming of the Holy Spirit. That is why the two men asked why they were looking to heaven. Jesus gave them all the tools they needed to proclaim the Gospel to the world. In the Gospel, Jesus told them: "Go, therefore, and make disciples of all nations." Once they received the Holy Spirit, they were to baptize people into the life, death, and resurrection of Jesus.

We are a mission church. Jesus has given us the same gifts he gave to his apostles. We can't spend our time looking into the sky looking for Jesus to return. We are not called to stand by in anticipation. We are called to make disciples of all nations. We are called to bring people to the waters of salvation. Jesus is the gift that we offer to the world. By our very baptism, we are Christ's disciples and as such sent forth to others. It is not enough to know about Jesus and all that he gave us; we must also actively live out the Gospel message.

The Ascension of the Lord calls us out of observation into becoming active people of God. We cannot be afraid to share our faith with others. Our actions should reflect a healthy understanding of what it means to be the Body of Christ. What we do for others should be a way of witnessing what it means to be a follower of Jesus. It is easy to stand on a mountain top and gaze into the sky, but that won't help in making disciples. Jesus demands more from us. Whether we pray for others, volunteer our time and resources, or give someone a shoulder to lean on for support, we are all called to be Christ for others.

While the Ascension is about Jesus returning to the right hand of God until he returns again, it is also about a beginning for his Church. While Jesus is no longer physically among us, we are truly his hands and feet. Be Christ for others. Make disciples of the world. Allow God to lead you to others and give them the gift of the risen Jesus.

PENTECOST

The Peace of Jesus

> "'Peace be with you. As the Father has sent me, so I send you.' And when he had said this, he breathed on them and said to them, 'Receive the Holy Spirit. Whose sins you forgive are forgiven them and whose sins you retain are retained.'"

Pentecost is a time when the Spirit, whom Jesus promised, was sent to the apostles. Jesus ascended into heaven and entrusted the Gospel into the apostles' hands. The birth of the Church begins at Pentecost.

This Gospel is taken from John. It gives a view of what happened on the evening of Easter. The disciples were locked away much in the same way they were on Pentecost. They were afraid of what might happen to them. Were they next to die? Would they be taken away as Jesus was? No wonder the first words out of Jesus' mouth were, "Peace be with you." Not once, but twice Jesus offers these words of encouragement.

Jesus came to send them into the world as the Father had sent him. He came to give them what he promised them: the Holy Spirit. As he breathed the Holy Spirit on them, he told them about dealing with sin. They had the power to forgive or not forgive sins.

The first assignment, if you will, was to try and heal people spiritually. If they saw a person who was contrite, they were to offer forgiveness. If a person wasn't sorry for their sins, then the sins remained. The disciples always had to remember to rely on the guidance of the Holy Spirit. Renewed with the Holy Spirit, they had the courage to go out into the world and share the Good News. Some fifty days after Easter, we see how the Spirit moved them to go out and preach. They spoke the universal words that came from Jesus. They no longer lived in fear but became bold and on fire with the love of Jesus. The beginning of the Church was to grow rapidly that day.

How are things with you and me? Have we left the upper room? Has the Spirit rushed through our lives and given us the courage to live out the Gospel? These are more than just nice stories that we can sit back and hear. We are also called to heal others. This is difficult to do if we have not felt the Lord's healing presence. Have we allowed Jesus to enter into our fears, the things that keep us locked away from the world? Jesus wants each of us to experience his peace. Jesus comes into our lives to breathe the Holy Spirit on us. Can we accept that gift? If we allow Jesus to heal us and make us whole, nothing should stop us from bringing that healing to others. Pentecost is a time for us to remember what Jesus has given us and how we are called to bring it to others. As the disciples had courage to go out into the world, may the Holy Spirit touch our lives in the same way. As we are forgiven, so we should forgive others.

TRINITY SUNDAY

The Unity of the Trinity

> "The grace of the Lord Jesus Christ and the love of God and the fellowship of the Holy Spirit be with you all."

These words are taken from the second reading on Trinity Sunday. Before the new Roman Missal, this was one of the options as a greeting to begin the Mass. I miss beginning Mass with these powerful words. Paul encourages the church in Corinth to use these words when greeting one another. It really speaks of the unity of the Trinity and how that unity brings a sense of wholeness to those who believe. Every time we make the sign of the cross, we are not only reminded of our baptismal promises but also the love that the Father, Son, and Holy Spirit brings to each of us.

As we hear in the Gospel, Jesus' mission here on earth was to show the love the Father had for us. He came into the world so that we might have eternal life. As Jesus walked the earth and began to open up the way to salvation, he gave us the gift of the Spirit. The Spirit is continuously revealing himself to us as we open up to his presence. Jesus not only gave us the gift of the Spirit but also the gift of himself. Through his death and resurrection, he opened the gates of heaven. Each time we receive the Eucharist, we are strengthened by his love and reminded of what he did for each of us.

God has given us so much. He created us out of love—in His image and likeness. Because of humanity's selfishness, we lost track of our life with God. We have created many gods in our world that distract us from God. The journey back to the Lord must be navigated with the help of Jesus, whose life reminds us once again of God's love. He shows us mercy, compassion, and forgiveness in our lives. He gave the people of God a way back to the Father, and it is up to us to believe in the path. It is the only way to avoid condemnation.

As we know, Jesus promised another Advocate to come as he returned to the right hand of the Father. Therefore, we have someone to defend us and guide us on our journey. Even if we drift off the path, God is there to put us back on the road. It would be great if we all greeted one another as Paul told the Corinthian community. A sense of peace comes over us when we hear those words. "The grace of the Lord Jesus Christ and the love of God and the fellowship of the Holy Spirit be with you all." This statement unites us. It lets us know we remain in the love of the Father, Son, and Holy Spirit.

THE FEAST OF CORPUS CHRISTI

The Greatest Gift

> Jesus said to them, "Amen, amen, I say to you, unless you eat the flesh of the Son of Man and drink his blood, you do not have life within you. Whoever eats my flesh and drinks my blood has eternal life, and I will raise him on the last day."

This Gospel passage is read when we celebrate the feast of The Most Holy Body and Blood of Christ, Corpus Christi Sunday. When you think about it, every time we celebrate Mass we are celebrating the Body and Blood of Christ. To be fed by Jesus is why we gather as a community. Receiving the Eucharist is one of the most powerful gifts that God has given us.

Jesus came into the world to bring us home to the Father. He gave his life so that we might all live. During the Last Supper, Jesus gave us his body and blood in the breaking of the bread and the blessing of the cup of wine. He told the apostles to celebrate that meal in remembrance of him. It united the early Christians as they came together the first day of the week to celebrate the life of Jesus.

Jesus gives us food for the journey—his body and blood is meant to sustain us. He gives us life from this meal and promises that we will be with him in the end. This should give us a sense of comfort and peace in our lives. We have life because of what Jesus has done for us. It is a life made stronger by our participation in the Eucharist. We should be so excited when it comes time to celebrate Mass. We should be so grateful that we have the privilege to receive Jesus in the Eucharist.

There are many reasons why I became a priest. I take presiding at Mass very seriously, and I feel so honored to lead a faith community to experience the true presence of Jesus in the Eucharist. Each Mass I celebrate, I try to bring into my homily something about the Eucharist. When we humbly come before the table of the Lord, our "Amen" states that we believe in what we receive. Our churches should be filled every week as we come to gather around the table of sacrifice. Unfortunately, that isn't always the case. Our numbers seem to drop when school comes to an end. I know people go on vacation, but it seems to happen every year.

If the Eucharist doesn't excite us, then we are missing one of the greatest gifts God has given us. On this feast of the Body and Blood of Christ, let us take a moment and say thanks to God for giving us his son, Jesus. Our path to the Father goes through Jesus. Jesus' Body and Blood give us life, life to the fullest. Praise God for loving us so deeply.

ORDINARY TIME

Jesus Within Us

> "John the Baptist saw Jesus coming toward him and said, 'Behold, the Lamb of God, who takes away the sin of the world...Now I have seen and testified that he is the Son of God.'"

We read this passage in ordinary time, a time to see the unfolding of Jesus' earthly mission. In today's Gospel, we hear of John's mission coming to an end. John has done what the Lord has asked of him; he identified the Lamb of God: Jesus, who is the Son of God.

Now it becomes our mission to identify Jesus in our lives. The baptism of repentance is now replaced with Jesus baptizing with the Holy Spirit. Have we experienced this baptism that Jesus gives? Can we see Jesus in our daily lives? Can we see him in one another? For many, the answer to these questions would be a firm "yes," but I wonder how well we recognize the "Lamb of God." When we go to church, do we feel the presence of Jesus in our liturgies? Do we see Jesus in our families? Do we see Jesus in others?

Jesus often gets lost in our world. Our life can be so one-dimensional. Jesus could walk right past us and we wouldn't recognize him because we are so into our own little worlds. We can also be very selective in where we see Jesus. When we're at Mass, do we really see the community of the Body of Christ? Better yet, do we truly believe that the bread and wine being offered at Mass *IS* the Body and Blood of Jesus? Sometimes it is difficult to tell if people believe when they come forward to receive the Eucharist.

If we receive Jesus into our lives, he should dwell within us. When we realize that Jesus is a part of us, that acknowledgement should make a big difference in how we look at others and how we look at ourselves. John the Baptist was guided by the Spirit when it came time for him to reveal Jesus to the world. That same Spirit calls us to the same revelation. Jesus is the Lamb of God who takes away the sin of the world.

I believe the sin John is referring to is the sin of pride. Pride keeps us from being humble before the Lord. Pride gets in the way of seeing Jesus in others. Pride holds us back from truly allowing Jesus to be a part of our lives. Once we put on the mantle of humility, we see the world differently. Our focus is now God-centered and not self-centered. When we allow the Lord to lead us and give us direction, we see the world from another set of eyes: God's. Jesus came to earth to show us the Father's love. He came to free us from sin. Free from sin, we can embrace the will of the Father. We can reveal God's love to others we encounter. Work on seeing Jesus, the Son of God, in the world. Allow him to show forth through you.

Go Fish!

> "Repent, for the kingdom of heaven is at hand…Come after me, and I will make you fishers of men."

Jesus picks up right where John the Baptist left off when he finished his ministry. Both called the people to repent. While John called for a change of heart for the coming of the Messiah, Jesus told them that the kingdom of heaven was at hand. For some, John's message was easier to understand; Israel had waited a long time for this Messiah to come. Jesus began to talk about the kingdom of heaven and not everyone in those days believed in a life after death. This talk of a new kingdom was not well received by all.

As Jesus began his mission, he did not make the journey alone. He reached out to simple men who had simple jobs: fishermen. He told them that if they follow him, they will be out to catch people. As I read the Gospel this week, I am struck by the mission of Jesus as he called others to join him. Once we have repented, it is not enough to say we are free of our sins. We must then accept the second part of the story. We are called to bring others to Jesus. We are to invite people to learn about the kingdom of heaven that is at hand.

How well are we doing? Attending Mass each week is a step. It is certainly a good start to begin each week receiving the Eucharist, but we have to do something with the Eucharist after we have received it. We have to make it alive in our lives. We have to be the ones who fish. This is a responsibility not just for the ordained, but for all baptized Christians. Life does not end with our life on earth. We will someday come to the end of this journey. We will be asked how well we have done with this life. It will not be enough to say, "I went to church every week."

When we embrace the teaching of Jesus, we are called to live a life that is kingdom bound. We, by our lives, have to witness to others that the love of God is alive and well in our lives. How we treat one another- including strangers- should reflect the love of God we have in our hearts. It takes a daily commitment to live as Christ called us to live. We are his disciples. He has given each of us gifts and talents to use for the building up of the kingdom. Jesus' mission should be our mission. If there are obstacles in our way, we should do whatever it takes to remove them. If sin is in the way, we need to repent. Jesus is calling us into the kingdom. We have tasted it in the sacramental life of the Church. We can experience it in our faith community, in our family, and at work or school.

Come be a disciple of Jesus and bring the kingdom of heaven to others!

Let Your Light Shine

> "You are the light of the world. A city set on a mountain cannot be hidden. Nor do they light a lamp and then put it under a bushel basket; it is set on a lampstand, where it gives light to all in the house."

I am sure this is a very familiar passage. It sounds so simple, so easy to follow. As you reflect on the words, what kind of light are you? A lot of people hide their light. Many people have such wonderful gifts from God but they don't share them. They spend a lot of time looking for the bushel basket to hide their light from people. Some people see others doing the work and think that everything is going just fine and that their input would not be seen as valuable. Those people are wrong. All of us have been given the light of Christ. At our baptism, we receive the light of Christ and are told to keep the flame burning. We can't sell ourselves short. We have to shine our light for the whole world to see.

> *"...Your light must shine before others, that they may see your good deeds and glorify your heavenly Father."*

When we work for the honor and glory of God, we are truly letting our light shine. As Jesus tells us, our good deeds keep the flame alive for others to see. This is not something that just a few are called to do. The

Lord has given us so much and we are called to respond with gratitude. We are to be about good deeds. In treating others with dignity, we acknowledge not only the light that burns in our lives, but we recognize the light of Christ burning in others. When we express our faith by treating others as if we are reaching out to Jesus, we have learned how to be a light for the world. When we reach out to those who need our help, Christ's light shines for all to see. We simply can't have the attitude of letting someone else take care of it. We are all in this together; we are a faith community.

Gathering for Sunday Mass reminds us that we are one body, led by the light of Jesus. We come to the altar to receive the Body and Blood of Jesus that gives us food for the journey. He gives of himself so that we might be filled with his love. In receiving his love we are called to share it with others. Through random acts of kindness we continue to give Christ to others. When our light is burning brightly, we can come to others and light the flames in their heart. What are you going to do this week to show your light to others? Jesus' light is among us; let us share that light.

People of Action

"Jesus said to his disciples: 'Do not think I have come to abolish the law or the prophets. I have come not to abolish but to fulfill. Amen, I say to you, until heaven and earth pass away, not the smallest letter or the smallest part of a letter will pass from the law, until all things have taken place. Therefore, whoever breaks one of the least of these commandments and teaches others to do so will be called least in the kingdom of heaven. But whoever obeys and teaches these commandments will be called greatest in the kingdom of heaven.'"

Some felt that Jesus came into this world to change everything about the law. Matthew's Gospel makes it evident that was not the case. Instead, Jesus gave us a deeper meaning and different perspective of the Ten Commandments. He calls us to see our neighbor in a different light. It takes hard work and grace to keep the commandments. If something gets in the way of obeying God, we must remove it from ourselves. Jesus told us that it is better to cut out an eye or cut off an arm and go to heaven then it is to not remove it and enter the gates of hell.

Once again, Jesus told us we can't be passive in our relationship with God and our neighbor. We will be judged by what we did or did not do in this world. If we refuse to listen to Jesus' words, we will find ourselves without a relationship with the Lord and that would be hell. We cannot simply give lip service to the Lord. We have to be people of action.

There is more to life than just Sunday Mass. There is only one God and he calls us to follow him with our whole being. We have to see one another as children of God. This means we must do a better job of respecting one another rather than judging one another. We are called to extend a hand in peace and not a fist in anger. Listen and follow the teachings of Jesus, who brings both the wisdom of the prophets and the sacred law Moses gave us.

The Gospel, which is taken from Jesus' Sermon on the Mount, is meant to challenge us. Are we ready to embrace Jesus' teachings? If we can obey, we are not far from the Kingdom. When we do obey, we are examples to others on following the Gospel's teachings. Let our actions reveal our love of God. Let us show our gratitude by opening our hearts to Jesus. He shows us the way to the Father. He shows us the attitude it takes to be his disciples. While following the laws he sets before us may seem overwhelming at times, they are guidelines established for our salvation. Let us surrender to the Lord.

God's Mercy and Compassion

> "...For if you love those who love you, what recompense will you have? Do not the tax collectors do the same? And if you greet your brothers only, what is unusual about that? Do not the pagans do the same? So be perfect, just as your heavenly Father is perfect."

We are still with Jesus as he continues to teach us from the Sermon on the Mount. Jesus continued to challenge us to be better people. He called for an effort that might take us out of our comfort zone. When we leave our comfort zones, there can be some real resistance. It is hard to reach out to people. The Master calls us to love our enemies and pray for those who persecute us. That's difficult, especially after they have hurt us. Many times we want to get even with people who hurt us, not love and pray for them as we should. Jesus calls us to use compassion. Once we have experienced his mercy toward us, we need to start extending it to others who need it too.

It is hard in the world we live in to be compassionate and merciful. We live in the "I" generation. We will go to extremes to protect our space. Society teaches us this behavior, but that is not how God wants us to live in the world. We are called to live as brothers and sisters—children of God. Anyone who has brothers and sisters knows there isn't always peace among them! There are some siblings who have not spoken to each other in years. The more we take hurts and resentments and lift them up in prayer, the better we all are. God doesn't ask us to forget what happens to us, but he does call us to let go of the situation. If hatred and anger are part of our daily lives, they will suck the very goodness we have out of our lives. The more we can learn about God's compassion and mercy, the freer we become.

We need to learn to be other-centered and not self-centered. That takes work on our part. It takes a good spiritual life and that really comes from how well we communicate with God. Have we felt the Lord's mercy and compassion in our own lives? Do we really know that the Lord forgives us when we turn to him? It is almost impossible to show mercy, compassion, and forgiveness when we haven't experienced it from God. We need to work on that. We need to practice forgiving others, not just the people we like or get along with.

The love of God is not selective; it is offered to all of us. Do we have the right to take that love away from others? *No!* Jesus challenges us again this week to live our faith. It has to be more than just words; it has to be a way of life. Let us all turn to the Lord for his guidance.

Seeking Out the Kingdom

"Your heavenly Father knows that you need them all. But seek first the kingdom of God and his righteousness, and all these things will be given to you besides. Do not worry about tomorrow, tomorrow will take care of itself. Sufficient for a day is its own evil."

I tend to worry a lot. As pastor, I look at the collections and worry about meeting our financial obligations. When we are down, that isn't a good sign. There tends to be a knot in my stomach as I think of meeting our budget. When I give homilies, I worry about being true to the Gospel. The Gospel is so rich each week and I feel blessed to share my thoughts on it.

What the Gospel tells me today is that there are many things out of our control. All the planning for the future may cause us not to focus on the here and now. Jesus offers us the Gospel and calls us to live it. How good are we at following his message? Are we people who seek out the kingdom? Are we working towards God's righteousness? It seems that these two things should take up a lot of energy and time, but God gives us all we need to fulfill these tasks. His love keeps us close to him, and he will not abandon us. We still have to give our best effort. We are called to use our time, talents, and treasures for the building up of the kingdom. We are called to treat one another with respect. These things need our energy.

In the beginning of the Gospel, Jesus tells us that we have to make a choice. We cannot serve two masters. We will either serve God or we will serve the material world and all its trappings. Which do we choose? We all want to serve the Lord, but how many of us are actually serving the material world? We want so much because we feel we have earned it. We think we need more stuff in our life. We need the fastest internet, the latest computer, a big-screen TV, and the list goes on. Will our material gains get us any closer to the kingdom of God? I really don't think they will.

Spend more time being good and faithful stewards. In gratitude, we should share with others as we give back to our Lord. Let's worry about our salvation and the salvation of others, not the small stuff. God knows what we need and will take care of us. If we trust in Him, we will work more in tune with living out the Gospel. We all have been called by Jesus to follow him. Let us be good stewards of the gifts that God has placed in our hands.

Reconnect With God

> "Come to me, all you who labor and are burdened, and I will give you rest. Take my yoke upon you and learn from me, for I am meek and humble of heart; and you will find rest yourselves. For my yoke is easy and my burden is light."

I love Jesus' words in this Gospel. If you are a believer in the Lord, you just feel better when hearing these words.

Sometimes in our daily lives, we start to feel like the world is sitting on our shoulders and weighing us down. You might have stress from work that you bring home at the end of the day. Your family seems to want more and more of your time and you don't know where that time will come from. Even the drive home can be a stressful situation. There are so many things that impact our daily lives, and all can seem to be a burden.

When we begin to feel like we are going it alone, we need to turn to the words of Jesus. His love can bring us peace. It should not be us against the world. We have a friend in Jesus. He is the source of comfort that we long for. He can show us another way to deal with the labor of the world.

So often we find ourselves too busy. When we become too busy for prayer—for connection with the Lord—we can quickly get lost. It's not that Jesus has gone anywhere, but rather that we have drifted off. We find ourselves taking on the world alone. You know the feeling: your patience runs thin and you find yourself blowing up at your family and friends. There is tightness in your chest as you try to hold it all together. Then, without warning, it all comes out.

We have to find that place where we can sit back, gather ourselves, and find some time to reconnect with God. God has big shoulders and a compassionate heart. He knows what we need before we ever come to ask for it, and he will wait for us to come to him. He will not force himself upon us.

Turn to Jesus and learn from him. He shows us his yoke is easy and his burden is light. When we surrender to Jesus and allow him to share our journey, the stress can begin to leave our lives. We all need the time and a place to take a step back from the busy world and allow ourselves to breathe again. We should find time every day to decompress—a time to spend with the Lord Jesus. It is a habit that can be rewarding and life giving.

We don't have to take on the world by ourselves. Jesus is willing to ease our burdens and teach us his ways. Let us turn to him and allow him to hold us in his loving arms. It is so refreshing when we do.

Life-Giving Soil

"Whoever has ears ought to hear...But the seed sown on rich soil is the one who hears the word and understands it, who indeed bears fruit and yields a hundred or sixty of thirtyfold."

The sower and the seed parable—a story we have often heard. The yield of sixty or thirtyfold is an unbelievable yield. Any farmer listening to Jesus would be in shock. It could only come from a soil that was enriched with the grace of God. We would all like to be the fruitful soil that Jesus describes in this parable. Jesus chose to make the mysteries of the Kingdom of Heaven known. It is a gift that Jesus planted within their hearts to grow and mature in their lives. The disciples had the ears to hear about salvation.

How do we get to the place where Jesus' disciples are in the Gospel? I am sure that at times during our life we have found ourselves in soil that isn't as life-giving as we would like it to be. Some of us have been in tough places and it seems that Jesus is not there for us. Perhaps we weren't listening; maybe we couldn't pick up the voice of Jesus trying to lead us to a better place. Jesus has offered to all who would listen to him the Kingdom of Heaven. When our hearts are in the right place, Jesus' voice is clear. When our hearts are being led astray, we are deaf. We sometimes find ourselves in a bad place—a place where the words of the Kingdom are muffled and distant. Many things in the world would like to draw us away. We have to remain strong and know that the words of the Lord will always lead us home. He calls us, and when we remain still, his words speak to our heart. The seed finds its roots in good soil where it can yield the harvest of sixty or thirtyfold.

When we find ourselves in soil that is not life-giving, we must find ways to reconnect with Jesus. We might have to reconcile with the Lord for drifting away. We might need to reconcile with one another when we are pushing away from the people who love us. Jesus' word remains constant as he shows us the way to the Father. Sometimes we just have to clean out the clutter that fills our ears. Don't let the noise of the world close you off to a relationship with the Lord, Jesus. We have to allow Jesus' words to be nurtured in our hearts so they can yield a bountiful harvest. Only a relationship with God can give us that joy. Whoever has ears ought to hear.

Hearing the Good News

"Whoever has ears ought to hear."

Once again, Jesus spoke to his disciples about the kingdom of heaven. He took the time to teach them the meaning of the parables. Why did Jesus only speak to them in parables? If you examine each of the parables told in today's Gospel, it seems that those in the crowd should have understood the metaphor. However, to say that is assuming the crowd knew of the kingdom of heaven. It's easy for us, as we look back at the stories, to understand that Jesus was telling us about the kingdom. For those in Jesus' time, they may not have fully understood the notion of the kingdom of heaven. We start to see that as Jesus took aside his disciples and broke open the parables.

Are we "kingdom aware"? Do we have the ears to hear what Jesus is offering us? The only way that we can truly prove that we "hear" what Jesus is saying is to live our lives in such a way that the kingdom is our mission. As the first parable tells us, there will be evil that grows side by side with us. With the help of Jesus, we can remain faithful to the kingdom and survive any and all temptations. When his angels come, the bad and the good will be separated. Those who have lived fulfilling the Gospel will find the kingdom of heaven waiting for them. Those who have embraced evil as their God will find themselves thrown into the fires of hell.

No one is free from the temptation of sin; it is all around us. There may be times when we fall into the temptation of sin, but Jesus always gives us a way back home. Through prayer, reconciliation, and the healing graces of God, we can be made whole. Those who endure the trials of this world will find favor with the Lord. As Jesus says in the Gospel, "Then the righteous will shine like the sun in the kingdom of their Father."

As we heard in the other two parables, it doesn't take much to make the kingdom of heaven grow. The smallest part of the Gospel has the potential to grow and expand throughout the world. We can do so much with what we have heard from the Lord. Sometimes we may never really know what impact we have on another person. It could be a small act of kindness, volunteering for a project, or praying for another who seems to have lost his or her way. There are so many opportunities to allow the kingdom to grow in us so that we might share in some way that gift with others.

Did you ever think that volunteering at church could be a way to spread the Good News? Jesus took the time to sit down with his disciples so that they could really understand what the kingdom of heaven is all about. Have our ears heard the same Good News? Only our lives will reveal how well we have heard. We are all called to be a part of the kingdom. Let us keep finding ways to make the kingdom come alive in our daily lives.

Saying Yes to Jesus

> "'Do you understand all these things?' They answered, 'Yes.' And he replied, 'Then every scribe who has been instructed in the kingdom of heaven is like the head of a household who brings from his storeroom both the new and the old.'"

In these last few passages, we have heard Jesus describing the kingdom of heaven. He cited many examples, and he spoke about the cost and how the kingdom should be the first priority in life. Sacrifices indeed must be made in order for us to be in Jesus' master plan. The information is overwhelming. It sounds so simple, but it's actually very challenging to be a part of the kingdom of heaven.

Jesus finally asked his disciples if they understood what he had told them. Of course they said they did—who would want to go against Jesus? However, Jesus told them that if they were wise they would do well to draw from the old: the Law of the prophets, and the new: the law of Jesus. Both the old and the new would serve them in understanding the concept of being a part of the kingdom of heaven. Jesus was teaching and preparing them for their mission to call others to what Jesus told them about salvation. As the disciples' answered *yes*, it began to sink into their hearts. They soon began to realize it was going to take much more than lip service to follow Jesus. As they began to take in what the teacher was saying, they learned that they would in turn have to teach others about the kingdom of heaven. They would have to make their commitment to Jesus the most important part of their lives, and their choice would eventually cost them their own.

These past few readings have been about the kingdom. When Jesus turns to you and asks if you understand what he has taught, what will your answer be? It is Jesus after all, how could we say anything but *yes*? But if we say *yes*, are we ready to accept the responsibilities that come with that response? Are we willing to move whatever gets in our way? Is the kingdom the treasure we have been seeking? Can we pay the price for the gift of salvation? If our answer is still *yes* to Jesus, it is going to take more than showing up for Mass on Sunday.

We have to be willing to live as active members of the kingdom. We have to be Christ for others. We have to find ways to focus on others rather than ourselves. Our attitude can't be one of, "just me and God." We have to find ways to show that God's love for us is shared with those around us. It should really begin at home with our family, but it has to go beyond them into the world around us. We are called to show the Lord's compassion and mercy. We begin to teach by example. The kingdom of heaven is already among us and we are called to build up the kingdom with grace of the Lord. We are kingdom people; let us act like it.

Excuses and Solutions

> "When it was evening, the disciples approached him and said, 'This is a deserted place and it is already late; dismiss the crowds so that they can go to the villages and buy food for themselves.' Jesus said to them, 'There is no need for them to go away; give them some food yourselves.'"

The disciples had an excuse for Jesus—they only had five loaves and two fish--and they could not possibly feed such a crowd. It is true: by themselves, they could not. But with the help of Jesus, the Son of God, they could and did feed well over 5,000 people. As a matter of fact, there were twelve baskets of leftovers after everyone had their fill.

Aren't we like the disciples? When we are faced with a challenge, we sometimes find any number of excuses not to face it. Many times we just figure someone else will take care of it. We may not be called to feed 5,000 people with five loaves and two fish, but there are many opportunities where we can make a difference. I look around at so many people who give their time and energy for the good of the parish family. When you take a careful look, many times it is the same group of people just wearing a different hat for a different project. I know that all of us are busy and have little time to give to our families, let alone to the parish and to the kingdom. However, if we all took that approach, our community would be hurting. The more people who can find time to give, the easier the load will be for all.

In today's Gospel, the disciples want the problem to go away. They were concerned with the crowds and it was a deserted place. Their way of solving the problem was to send them away, but Jesus made them look into themselves and see another possibility. Jesus took what gifts they had, blessed and broke them, and began to share with the community. Jesus cured the sick and he satisfied their hunger. Not only did he satisfy the physical hunger but also the spiritual hunger was taken care of that day. Jesus showed the disciples that much can be accomplished with the simple gifts they offered. Jesus showed them, with the help of God, they could bring peace and comfort.

We are challenged to use the gifts that have been placed in our care. Whether it is time, talent, or treasure, God expects us to give to the building up of the kingdom. There are many options to do this: feeding the hungry, bringing clothing for those in need, or finding time to help out in a parish project. There are many ways of lending a hand in our parishes and communities. Many helping hands make the burden so much lighter. Be one of those giving people, even though you might think you're too busy. We are truly blessed, and we can always work harder to serve as Christ calls us to.

Out of the Boat

> "'Lord, if it is you, command me to come to you on the water.' He said, 'Come.' Peter got out of the boat and began to walk on the water toward Jesus. But when he saw how strong the wind was he became frightened; and beginning to sink, he cried out, 'Lord, save me!' Immediately Jesus stretched out his hand and caught Peter, and said to him, 'O you of little faith, why did you doubt?'"

In a small prayer room I have in my home, among many pictures is the one of Peter walking on the water. Jesus is standing before him with his hand outstretched. I look at this picture often. I like Peter, and I believe we all have a little bit of him in our own lives.

In the story, Peter was the only one who left the boat. He was the only one who recognized Jesus, and his trust carried him toward Jesus on the water. The sea was rough, yet when Peter kept his eyes focused on the Lord, his strong faith persevered. But when Peter took in all that was around him, all that was out of his control, he doubted. When doubt took over, he simply began to sink. He cried out to the only one he knew could save him. It was not the last time Peter looked to Jesus for help. Jesus loved Peter and wanted to cure those doubts that Peter had in his life.

Sooner or later we all reach the point where we have to choose to stay in the boat or get out and reach out to the Lord. This is a great Gospel for people on retreat. Somewhere during the retreat experience, you come to the moment when the choice becomes all yours. Like in the Gospel, Jesus will be right there with you the whole time if you choose to leave the boat. Even if we have just enough faith to take that first step and then begin to sink, Jesus won't let go of us. When we stay focused on Jesus and look into his loving eyes, we grow stronger in our faith, in our security to walk on the water.

Once we find ourselves in the hands of the Lord, there is a sense of serenity in our lives. We are made whole and we grow stronger in our faith. We can be a source of strength for others to venture out of the boat, even if they feel terrified and lost. We can show others how reaching out to the Lord can bring them peace. Once we find ourselves in the loving arms of the Lord, we can find peace.

We all can recognize that Jesus is truly the Son of God. When Jesus is the focus of our lives we can weather any storm that comes over us. Jesus never leaves us alone; he will always be the hand that saves us from sinking. With Jesus as our source of life, we can always have the faith that keeps us strong in the world.

We're all God's Children

> "And behold, a Canaanite woman of that district came and called out, 'Have pity on me, Son of David! My daughter is tormented by a demon.' …Then Jesus said to her in reply, 'O woman, great is your faith! Let it be done for you as you wish.' And the woman's daughter was healed from that hour."

The narrator wants us to know this is no ordinary woman, but a Canaanite woman. The disciples want Jesus to send her away and feel that she is unworthy of their time. Jesus seems to agree with his disciples. He tells her he was sent only to the lost sheep of the house of Israel.

This sure doesn't sound like the merciful, compassionate Jesus I thought I knew! When the woman continued her plea, Jesus said in reply: "It is not right to take food of the children and throw it to the dogs." Wow! Jesus seemed to be reacting just the way his disciples hoped he would. They thought they should let her find help among her own people. But in the Gospel, that isn't really how Jesus deals with people. Jesus was amazed at her faith and granted the healing of her daughter. He indeed had taken pity on her. Were the disciples disappointed, or were their eyes opened to see that compassion belongs to all of God's people?

In Matthew's Gospel, there is a focus on the "lost sheep of the house of Israel." The author wanted the first opportunity to embrace the "New Moses," as Jesus was called. It did not mean that the Gospel was only for them; the gospel was to be universal, open for all to accept. However, it is easy to see how that notion of exclusion caught on.

We as Catholics can sometimes be exclusive in our ways of treating people, but we are truly not alone in this. Other religions can have the same type of attitude. It's easy to fall back on familiar habits when we are around others whom we believe are unlike us. We may believe that people who aren't like us aren't our problem. This is the disciples' attitude: in their minds, the Canaanite woman was not their problem. They wanted to send her away so they could go on with their mission; out of sight, out of mind. Jesus had much to teach them about their mission's purpose.

Jesus saw the Canaanite woman's faith. This is what he looks for in each one of us. He looks at our core, the essence of who we are, and challenges us to do the same with others. We need to let go of our judgmental side. We have to see the person that is before us. We have to learn how to respect each human being. This is lacking in our world today. We are responsible for taking care of each other. We must not push people aside and say they're someone else's problem. We can't say that they are not one of us. In the eyes of God, we are all his children, so let us act that way!

Who is Jesus?

"Jesus said to them, 'But who do you say that I am?' Simon Peter said in reply, 'You are the Christ, the Son of the living God.' Jesus said to him in reply, 'Blessed are you, Simon son of Jonah. For flesh and blood has not revealed this to you, but my heavenly Father.'"

Jesus wanted to know how people saw him. He first asked what other people had to say about him. Then Jesus looked to his disciples and asked them who *they* said he was. By the grace of God, Peter was able to proclaim Jesus' true identity. Jesus praises Peter for the answer and tells Peter he is the rock on which he is going to build his church, but he then tells the disciples to tell no one of this revelation. Why? It is because each of us has to have that revelation touch our own heart. When Jesus becomes real to us in our faith life, only then can we see him as the Son of God.

"Who do you say that I am?"

It is a question that only some of us dare to ask, but most of us would love to know the answer. Most people know you by your actions, your job, whether you are married or not, children or no children, where you live, and things like that. However, these details aren't the entirety of who you are, and sometimes others can never seem to capture the real you. They may only see what is on the outside.

When Jesus first asked the disciples about what they had heard from others, they were able to identify key figures that they experienced in the past. Most of them would have had a vivid view of John the Baptist. Many of them may have even seen John up close and personal. They knew of many of the prophets from the past, and Jesus must have fit their image, but Jesus wanted to know how his own followers felt. For the moment, Peter gave the right answer. He was in touch with the grace of the Father.

"Who do you say that I am?"

Jesus is asking each of us this question. There may be as many responses to this question as there are people who answer it. We all come to know Jesus at different times. For some, he might be seen as the Son of God, the Christ. Others might still be forming an idea of who he is and how he fits into their lives. As we will read later in the same chapter of Matthew, Peter quickly loses sight of who Jesus is; he stumbles when he speaks about what Jesus should do or not do in his life. We have to revisit the question a lot in our lives. Jesus doesn't just pose it to us once; it's a question we might have to answer every day.

If our answer is that Jesus *is* the Son of God, then it must be backed up with action. Jesus calls for more than a verbal response from us; he wants us to act on our answer. We are called to reveal to others this Jesus we have come to know. So let us bring others to Him.

Obstacles or Believers

> "Then Peter took Jesus aside and began to rebuke him, 'God forbid, Lord! No such thing shall ever happen to you.' He turned and said to Peter, 'Get behind me, Satan! You are an obstacle to me. You are thinking not as God does, but as human beings do.'"

Wow, what a difference a few verses make in the story of Peter! Not too long ago we heard Jesus praising Peter for recognizing that Jesus was the Christ, the Son of God. But when Jesus told his disciples what the Son of God must do, Peter wanted to protect Jesus. This is a noble act indeed, but Peter was no longer guided by the insight God had given him. He was thinking in human terms. Jesus called Peter an obstacle to him, and he told him to get out of the way, for his mission would not be denied. He would travel to Jerusalem where indeed a brutal death awaited him. Peter only sees the pain and suffering and not the bigger picture. Only later would Peter and the others learn what all of this would mean.

Jesus goes further in the Gospel and challenges all of his disciples. They are called to take up their cross and follow him. To be a follower of Jesus, one must deny him or herself; they have to let go of their life and embrace the power of God. There is a movement from self-centeredness to being other-centered. Peter failed to hear that there was salvation beyond the pain and suffering. Jesus was to be raised on the third day, shattering death's power over the world. Jesus knew his journey must end in Jerusalem. The disciples weren't ready for that news so they tried to change the subject.

I wonder how many times we have been an obstacle to Jesus. Perhaps we've been an obstacle when we've had our own agenda and tried to tell God what the plan should be. It's easy to fall into a rut and only focus on our little world.

Have we heard Jesus' words in our lives? How those words that Jesus spoke to Peter must have stung him. Have we failed to take up our cross and follow Jesus? I am guilty of preventing God's way from being my way. It is easy to let go of your cross and not follow Jesus, or to change the subject, but who are we fooling? When Jesus comes at the end of time, our lives will be an open book to him. Jesus will look at our lives and know whether or not we carried our cross. He will know if we have been an obstacle to his mission.

It's not too late! We don't have to go it alone. Jesus is always there to help us carry our cross. He will help us let go of our selfish ways and become a better person. What a loving, awesome God we have. Let us share that with others around us.

The Power of Prayer

> "...Again, amen, I say to you, if two of you agree on earth about anything for which they are to pray, it shall be granted to them by my heavenly Father. For where two or three are gathered together in my name, there I am in the midst of them."

What a wonderful gift the power of prayer can be in our lives. In the last couple of months, I have had the opportunity to offer the sacrament of anointing of the sick to several people of the parish. It is always special when there are others who join in the sacrament and lay hands on the person we are about to anoint. I can just feel the energy among the group gathered as we pray.

The last several anointed have been people preparing for surgery. The days leading up to surgery can be stressful times, but when people pray over the person, there is a sense of peace that comes only from prayer. I know from my own experience with surgeries that being prayed over and anointed gave me comfort.

When you experience the power of prayer in your life, it can connect you to the Lord. Obviously praying over a person is not the only way we can see prayer at work. We have an awesome prayer chain at our parish that takes the needs of people and lifts them up to God. People really depend on these powerful prayers when they or family members are in need.

But perhaps the most familiar way we see "where two or three are gathered in my name," is when we gather around the altar to celebrate the Eucharist. We all come together to join in a common prayer that we lift up to God. When we gather for Mass, each of us may come with a different purpose, but we are all unified by the Body and Blood of Jesus. While we all might seem different, we are still one in Jesus.

Jesus meets us where we are when we pray. He doesn't have a mysterious agenda we have to figure out before he will listen to us; he knows our hearts. When a community, no matter how small or large, comes together for prayer, Jesus is in our midst. When we offer our petitions to the Lord, we know he hears us and will give us what we need.

The power of prayer is amazing. It can unify a community and teach us how to be Christ to one another. Jesus knows that we need him, but it is nice when we actually ask him for the help. He repeatedly calls us to be a part of his life, but we must remember that while we are encouraged to ask, we also must show our gratitude to the Lord. We must always remember that we have so much to be thankful for: so many gifts given to us by the Father. We are so blessed when we are a part of a strong faith community. Let us give thanks to God. Let our prayer be one unto the Lord.

God's Generosity

> "...'My friend, I am not cheating you. Did you not agree with me for the usual daily wage? Take what is yours and go. What if I wish to give this last one the same as you? Or am I not free to do as I wish with my money? Are you envious because I am generous?' Thus, the last will be first, and the first will be last."

Here we read the parable of the landowner and the laborers. Jesus told us that their story is like the kingdom of heaven. Laborers who were hired first were upset that the ones who worked only an hour got the same wages they did for working a full day. They grumbled because they felt they should get more, but the landowner pointed out that all agreed on the daily wage and there was nothing unfair about how he treated those laborers who worked a full day.

Like the first laborers, we sometimes feel a sense of entitlement in our life with God. After all, we were baptized, we go to Mass (most of the time), and of course we love God. However, life in the kingdom isn't a job. God's gift of being with him is just that: a gift. We cannot earn our way into heaven. We don't earn bonus points for doing something nice for someone. In reality, that is what we are called to do if we embrace our faith. Jesus showed us how to live and how to treat one another. When we gather for Eucharist, it should not be out of a sense of obligation, but because it gives us life. Our joining for Mass is a time to say thank you to God for the blessings we have.

The landowner showed how generous he was with his money. Everyone who worked for him that day was paid the same wage. Like the landowner, God is generous with his love. Not everyone comes to a relationship with God at the same time. For some, being a part of God's family began as an infant. Others found their relationship with God later in life. The timing isn't really important. What is important is the realization that all have an opportunity to accept the grace of God. Therefore, instead of feeling upset or jealous of God's generosity, we should rejoice that other brothers or sisters have accepted the loving graces of God in their lives.

We are all called to work for the kingdom. We are to take our gifts, talents, and treasures and use them for the building up of the kingdom. We should see the example of God's generosity as a model for our own lives. We should want to share our lives with others. It is not a way to earn heaven or God's affection, for those things have already been given to us with no strings attached. Jesus clearly shows us the way to the

Father, the pathway to the kingdom. When we are called to work for the landowner, no matter when we get the call, we should accept the opportunity to work for the Master. As we gather to receive the Body and Blood of Jesus, may it fill our lives with his love so that we can be the people God calls us to be.

Which Child Are You?

> "Jesus said to them, 'Amen, I say to you, tax collectors and prostitutes are entering the kingdom of God before you. When John came to you in the way of righteousness, you did not believe him; but tax collectors and prostitutes did. Yet even when you saw that, you did not later change your minds and believe him.'"

Jesus spoke to the chief priests and elders of the people. He posed a simple question to them: Which son did the father's will? They knew the answer immediately because it was made obvious to them. Perhaps they were better off not answering Jesus' question, because he took the answer and turned it against them. He told the chief priests and elders that sinners were making it to the kingdom while they remained blind to the truth.

We might sit back and say, "What does this have to do with me?" While we are surely not chief priests or elders, we still have to take a hard look at what kind of children we are. If we are called to go and work in the vineyard, how do we respond? Some people respond and say "no" because they are too busy or don't feel they can make a difference. Some people pretend that they haven't heard the call of the Lord.

Perhaps they have hardened their hearts and feel unworthy to respond to the Lord. Then there are those who, for one reason or another, experience an awakening and realize that they must respond to the call.

Look who Jesus said was entering the kingdom: sinners. Jesus reminded the leaders of those who heard John and repented for the wrong they had done. He exposed their blindness. The chief priests and elders represent everyone who will not recognize Jesus in the world, and there are still many today who are blinded to the pathway to the kingdom of heaven.

There are many people in our world like the second son. They put on a good front for everyone to see but they sit in judgment of others and feel that saying *yes* is all that is necessary in response to God. In reality, God knows the hearts of each one of us. Because He knows our true responses, we can't hide from Him. He is there to hold up a mirror so that we might truly see who we are.

Fortunately, like in the Gospel, we always have an opportunity to change our ways. We can discover that saying *yes* to God is life-giving for us. When we see the mistakes we have made in our lives, we can return to the Lord. God calls each of us. He wants to be a part of our lives. God wants us to be his sons and daughters forever. When the Lord calls us to go out and work in the vineyard, what will our responses be? May we all respond with a resounding *yes* and support that response with our actions. We're all sinners and we all make mistakes, but the Father is always there to heal us and make us whole.

Sharing Our Rich Harvest

> Jesus said to them, "Did you never read in the Scriptures: The stone that the builders rejected has become the cornerstone; by the Lord has this been done, and it is wonderful in our eyes! Therefore, I say to you, the kingdom of God will be taken away from you and given to a people that will produce its fruit."

Jesus told the chief priests and the elders of the people a parable of a landowner and his tenants. In that parable, Jesus explained that the tenants had failed the landowner just as the chief priests and elders have failed to be good stewards of what God had entrusted with them.

The leaders thought only of themselves and not of the people the Lord asked them to lead. When it came time to share their produce, they became greedy. In the parable, when the greed showed its ugly self, the tenants killed the servants sent by the Master. Looking at the history of God's chosen ones, they failed time and again to listen to God's messengers. While prophets and judges tried to set things right with the Lord, the people rejected God's guidance.

Jesus is holding up a mirror to the leaders of the time. God offered them the best He had to give them: His Son. Like other messengers sent by God, he too was rejected and killed. Jesus told them that they have not chosen correctly. God would punish those who have turned their face away from Him. Greed and power would be their downfall. The tenants in the story were disrespectful and ungrateful to the landowner. He had given them everything necessary to have a rich harvest, yet they refused to give back to the landowner what was rightfully his.

While this story is directed to chief priests and elders, its telling is also for our benefit. God has given us everything we need to live in this world but have we been good stewards? Have we shown our gratitude for the many blessings God has given to us?

I'll admit I can find myself a bit greedy and selfish in my own life. I catch myself feeling a sense of entitlement. When I recognize this is wrong, I know that I need to refocus my life and appreciate what I have. Everything we have is a gift from God. We are able to support ourselves because of the talents God has given to each of us. We shouldn't wait for the Lord to ask for His own fruit. We should be willing to offer back to the Lord our best to show our gratitude for His love.

We have to make sure we aren't just takers in this world. We have to be givers as well. If we have an understanding of how blessed we are in our lives, we should want to share it with others. We must recognize the Son that God has sent to us for our salvation. When we are Christ to one another, that realization comes alive in our hearts. Let us be thankful for what the Lord has given us.

To Be Chosen

"The king said to him, 'My friend, how is it that you came in here without a wedding garment?' But he was reduced to silence. Then the king said to his attendants, 'Bind his hands and feet, and cast him into the darkness outside, where there will be wailing and grinding of teeth.' Many are invited, but few are chosen."

In this parable, a man was walking out on the street and he suddenly found himself at a wedding feast for the king's son. The king came in to greet the guests, and he singled out this man for not wearing a wedding garment. The man was suddenly thrown out into the street, rejected by the king. Again, Jesus was telling this parable to the chief priests and elders of the people. They have been the focus of Jesus' preaching for the last several Gospel passages.

God continues to offer the gift of salvation throughout the history of the Jewish people. Their leaders were not faith-filled people. They, in their arrogance, did not speak in the name of the Lord. In many ways, they made themselves the focus of faith.

We read earlier that tax collectors and prostitutes were entering the kingdom of heaven before the chief priests and the elders of the people. The ones who thought they had the inside track to a relationship with God failed to make the party because they were blind.

In this Gospel we find a similar story. In the beginning of the parable, the king was ready to celebrate the wedding feast. He joyfully sent out his servants to call the invited guests to the feast, but they refused his invitation. Refusing to give up, the king sent other servants to bring the guests to the feast. Their response was brutal: those invited destroyed the servants. Not only did they reject the invitation, but they also responded in violence. The feast was ready, so others must be called. They filled the room and the feast could finally begin. The guests were bad and good alike—those seemingly the least likely to attend the feast were there.

Jesus told us that many are indeed called, even those who appear to be imperfect. But even if we accept the call, we have to have the proper "wedding garment" to enter the kingdom. We need to turn our lives over to God. We have to allow him to heal us and make us whole. We need more than to be baptized and show up for Mass. God's graces must flow into our lives, and we have to continually renew our relationship with Him. Jesus came into this world to call us to the feast. His Father has made all the preparations.

The question for us then, is what will our response be when the Lord comes and calls us? Will we recognize the opportunity to follow, or will we simply say, "Not now, I'm too busy."? God will continue to call us to himself, but we still have to accept that call and we have to be dressed for the occasion. If we have not let go of our brokenness and accepted God's forgiveness, we may find ourselves thrown out into the darkness, "where there will be wailing and grinding of teeth." Pray for one another to be one of the chosen.

What Belongs to God

> "'Show me the coin that pays the census tax.' Then they handed him the Roman coin. He said to them, 'Whose image is this and whose inscription?' They replied, 'Caesar's.' At that he said to them, 'Then repay to Caesar what belongs to Caesar and to God what belongs to God.'"

In this Gospel, when the Pharisees tried to entrap Jesus in speech, we are told that Jesus knew the Pharisees' malice. It must have been difficult for Jesus, knowing that people tried to trick him and make him look bad. However, time and time again, the malicious leaders failed in their efforts to tear down Jesus.

Notice that Jesus did not avoid the question posed to him: "Is it lawful to pay the census tax to Caesar or not?" He knew well that the Roman government had requirements that the people must follow. The people owed money—whether they liked it or not—to those who ruled over them. Jesus' answer was simple: Give what belongs to Caesar back to Caesar. He didn't judge the fairness of the tax, but he told them that if they were going to live in this world, then they would have to obey the earthly rulers.

While Jesus had no issue with the taxes the leaders were talking about, he said there was a second half to the issue. Not only were they to repay Caesar, but they were commanded to give to God what belonged to God. While there may have been ways to cheat the taxes, it was impossible to cheat God. Is there anything that doesn't belong to God? My response to that question is that evil doesn't belong to God. God didn't create evil; it belongs to human beings.

So how well are we doing with giving to God what belongs to Him? How do we actually give back to God? When we use the gifts, talents, and treasures for the building up of the kingdom, we are giving back to God. When we respect the world that he gave us and are good stewards of this precious land, we are giving back to God.

We are to show gratitude for what has been placed into our hands. We need to show God that we want to be a part of the kingdom. We are called to take part in the mission of reaching out to others. It is time for us to serve others. Our whole lives should be giving back to God what belongs to Him. We can't be ungrateful takers because we think we deserve what we have or that we've earned it. It is our responsibility to be good and faithful stewards of the world and the people in it.

While we have to repay to Caesar what is owed to Caesar, our greater responsibility is giving back to God. We must always find ways to do that. Prayer can be a big part of our discovering what we are called to do. Come together to receive the Eucharist so we are nourished for our journey. We are all called to show our gratitude to the Lord with our lives. When we realize it is God who is in charge and has the ultimate plan, then we can do a better job of giving to God what belongs to Him.

The Greatest Commandment

"You shall love the Lord, your God, with all your heart, with all your soul, and with all your mind. This is the greatest and the first commandment. The second is like it: You shall love your neighbor as yourself. The whole law and the prophets depend on these two commandments."

Here, the Pharisees sent a scholar of the law to test Jesus. In this attempt to manipulate Jesus, the scholar wanted to know the greatest commandment out of the hundreds. Jesus did not hesitate with his answer; he passed the scholar's test. Now that we know the answer, what does it mean for you and me?

Jesus gave the scholar the two commandments because it is impossible to follow the first commandment without the second. In 1 John 4:20, we read: "If anyone says, 'I love God,' but hates his brother, he is a liar; for whoever does not love a brother whom he has seen cannot love God whom he has not seen. This is the commandment we have from him: whoever loves God must also love his brother." This makes sense and reminds us that saying we love God has to be backed up with the same action toward our neighbor.

God first loved us. He has filled us with his unconditional love that completes the very being of who we are. The only way we can respond to this love is to reach out to others and share what God has given us. The more we experience the love of God, the more we desire to share that love. When we reach out to others, we allow the love of God to flow out of us into them. This can sometimes be more challenging than it sounds.

The second commandment says we should love our neighbor as ourselves. This implies that we see ourselves as loveable, that we recognize God's love in us, and we accept that love. If we don't see ourselves as loveable, it is difficult to love anyone else. There has to be a source of love that we can tap into. If we feel unloved, we become a lost soul searching for meaning.

At an Archdiocesan Summit on the New Evangelization, the key note speaker, Bishop Frank Joseph Caggiano, said a common problem for people is that they don't believe they are lovable or loved. I agree that many people seem to struggle with this, and because of that, the two great commandments may seem impossible.

We are called to bring the love of Christ to others, to let them know they are loveable in the eyes of God, and to help them see the love that God has given them. It is in reaching out to them that we are true to the two commandments that Jesus gave the scholar.

Will we always be successful in giving this love? I'm sure we will stumble from time to time, but we must always remember that God's love is unconditional and will never be taken away from us. Let us learn to love our neighbors as if they are God himself.

Good and Faithful Servants

> "Then the one who had the one talent came forward and said, 'Master, I knew you were a demanding person, harvesting where you did not plant and gathering where you did not scatter; so out of fear I went off and buried your talent in the ground. Here it is back.'"

In this parable, a man entrusts his servants with his possessions according to their ability. The first two servants double what is given to them and return a profit back to their master. The last servant returns only the single talent. Fear drives this servant to bury his talent in the ground.

This parable reminds me of my grandparents. When I was growing up, I spent many a Saturday night with my grandma and grandpa. On Sunday morning, we would all go to church at their parish. They had a large house with plenty of property to explore and they often joked about burying coffee cans of money in the backyard. They grew up in a time when putting money in the bank was not the wisest thing to do. As a child, when I was out in the yard, I'd wonder just where they might have buried a coffee can or two full of money. When grandma moved, I thought about all the cans in the yard she left behind.

While my grandparents were only joking, there are some who do bury their talents out of fear. As we see in the parable, fear is not the best way to approach God. If the only reason we do or do not do something is because we are afraid of going to hell, we may not be living life to the fullest. As the master points out to the servant with talent, it would have been better to have placed the talent in the bank where it could have gained interest.

God has given talents to each of us according to our abilities. We are to take those talents and put them to good use and they will increase. When we put our talents to good use, we are being good stewards with what God has placed in our care. But if we bury our talents out of fear of losing it, losing it is exactly what happens.

When God comes to judge us, He will see how well we have used what He has placed in our care. If fear has dominated our choices, we can't be good stewards. Jesus tells the parable to remind the disciples of what will soon be theirs. He entrusts to them the church and all its members. They are called to carry on his mission: to be good stewards. They continued to pass the mission on to others as the church continued to grow.

Each of us is part of that same mission. We are to be good stewards of the kingdom. When the master returns, we will be called to settle our accounts. Will we be those who use our talents to make more, or will be the ones who, out of fear, do nothing with the talents? If we have chosen wisely, we will hear the Lord say: "Well done, my good and faithful servant…Come, share your master's joy."

SOLEMNITY OF SAINTS PETER AND PAUL

Leaders

> "And so I say to you, you are Peter, and upon this rock I will build my Church, and the gates of the netherworld shall not prevail against it."

> "I, Paul, am already being poured out like a libation, and the time of my departure is at hand. I have competed well; I have finished the race; I have kept the faith."

Here we celebrate Saints Peter and Paul, Apostles. We remember the wonderful gift these two were for our Church. Peter, a fisherman, and Paul, a tent maker, received the call from Jesus to preach the Good News. Peter was one of the first apostles who, inspired by the Father, proclaimed that Jesus was, "the Christ, the Son of the living God." He, with the other apostles, learned from the Master. Peter grew in his faith and became the leader of the early Church. He is the "rock" that Jesus used as the foundation. Peter was the one given the keys to the Kingdom of Heaven, but he had to follow God's guidance. Only through Him could salvation take place.

Paul was sent to the world of the Gentiles. Before his conversion, he was known as Saul, a Pharisee. He began his journey setting out to destroy the early Church, but Jesus had other plans for him. Called to change his life, Paul embraced the Good News of Jesus. It was the Lord who gave him strength to be able to preach and share Jesus with the world. The second reading speaks about Paul coming to the end of his journey. He had finished the race. Paul gave his life for the building up of the kingdom among the Gentiles.

It was Peter who defended Paul when it came to requirements for a Gentile to convert. It was not necessary for them to be Jewish first, and then become Christian. All were seen as equal by the early Church. Each was to be baptized in the name of the Father, Son, and Holy Spirit. They were all called to the same table to receive the Body and Blood of Jesus. The mission of Jesus was to the entire world, not just a select group.

As we celebrate this feast of Peter and Paul, we continue to see the influence they had on the Church. We have been blessed with many Spirit-filled leaders in our Church. What a wonderful leader we have in our current pope, Pope Francis. We trust that all our leaders are guided by the same Spirit that called these apostles to their journey of faith.

May we also depend on the guidance of Jesus in our daily lives. God has given us the same call to build up the Kingdom of Heaven. Are we willing to stand up for our faith and make a difference? Because of their faith in God, Peter and Paul laid the foundation for our Church. Let's give thanks for those leaders who have gone before us. Let us also pray for those leaders given the privilege to lead us in the world today. May God's spirit continue to guide them.

THE EXALTATION OF THE HOLY CROSS

The Power of the Cross

"And just as Moses lifted up the serpent in the desert, so must the Son of man be lifted up, so that everyone who believes in him may have eternal life."

In this Gospel, Jesus spoke to Nicodemus, a Pharisee. Jesus tried to teach him about the plan for salvation that the Father has in store for us. Out of love, God sent his only Son into the world. It is by this gift that God brings salvation to all who believe in the Son. If one believes in Jesus and his message, he or she shall live forever.

In celebrating the Exaltation of the Holy Cross, the Church wants us to remember always that the cross is a part of our faith. In the Gospel we read earlier, Jesus challenged us to pick up our own cross and follow him. Our salvation must go through the suffering and death of Jesus because we can't celebrate the resurrection without first going to Calvary. Just as healing was given to the Israelites in the desert when Moses mounted a seraph on a pole, the Son of Man will also be hung on a tree for the world to be healed.

The cross represents so much to our faith. The fact that Jesus was sent by his Father out of love should draw us closer to the cross. Each and every time we make the sign of the cross it should remind us of the love Jesus has for us.

Several years ago, there was a push by the Church to make sure that there was a cross with a corpus on it. A number of churches had the resurrected Jesus on the cross. Some had on one side the empty cross and next to it the resurrected Jesus. While the intent of the churches was to show the whole cross and resurrection connection, it took away from the moment of Jesus' suffering and death. When I spend time in my church, I am drawn to our cross because the image of Jesus is striking. When I look at Jesus on the cross, I realize how much he loves us and wants us to be a part of his life. What he endured for our sake is humbling. How could we ever turn away from a God who has given us so much?

Every time we gather for Eucharist we are called back to the cross. We remember what Jesus did for us. It is important that we see salvation in all that it entails— the suffering and the glory.

> *"For God so loved the world that he gave his only Son, so that everyone who believes in him might not perish but might have eternal life."* ~John 3:16

Jesus is a gift that God has given us and we are called to be grateful.

ALL SOULS' DAY

Remembering

> "And this is the will of the one who sent me that I should not lose anything of what he gave me, but that I should raise it on the last day."

This Gospel is read for All Souls' Day, a day when we remember the family and friends who have gone before us. We pray that they are with our heavenly Father in the kingdom of heaven. This passage is very familiar to me. Whenever I do a grave-site ceremony, I begin the service with these words. It reminds all of us that if we believe, then we belong completely to the Father. The Father has entrusted each of us into the hands of Jesus. Jesus' mission here on earth was to do the will of the Father and teach us about the love of God. When we begin to feel God's love in our hearts, we can really see our faith in Jesus grow.

Jesus has a promise for each of us: He will not lose anything the Father has given to him. The goal of Jesus' mission is to raise us all on the last day, and we hear this message at our baptism. We are welcomed into the life, death, and resurrection of Jesus. We become a part of God's family. As the perfect parent, the Father protects us and guides us with his mercy and compassion.

While this should bring comfort to us all, we still may experience fear or uncertainty when someone we know and love dies. Death is final in the earthly sense, but we were never created to live our life away from the Father. By Jesus' death and resurrection, the finality has been broken. As Jesus ascends into heaven, we know that one day we too shall join Jesus in our Father's house. This is something we have to hold onto when death impacts our family and friends.

Our prayers on All Souls' Day remind us of the certainty of death. Sometimes we might feel that we prayed harder for someone who died than we did when the person was alive. Remember that we are always called to pray for one another, living or dead. We pray that those who died are people who came to believe in God.

Despite the mess that the world throws at us, we still have Jesus offering himself to us. In the Eucharist, he reminds us that he will be our strength. Today we reflect on the lives of those we know who have left this earthly world. It is also a time for us to reflect on seeing Jesus as the source of eternal life. May we all one day be reunited with those who have gone before us at the banquet of the Lord.

CHRIST THE KING

The Least Ones

> "And the king will say to them in reply, 'Amen, I say to you, whatever you did for one of the least brothers of mine, you did for me…Amen, I say to you, what you did not do for one of the least ones, you did not do for me.' And these will go off to eternal punishment, but the righteous to eternal life."

This passage from Matthew's Gospel really makes me stop and think. We learn the judgment of humanity is based on not only what we do for people but also what we fail to do. Who are the "least ones" Jesus is talking about? How often have we passed up opportunities to help someone out?

Earlier, we read how Jesus explained the two great commandments: love God with your whole being, and love your neighbor as yourself. Jesus began to open the eyes of the people to see that more than just a select few should get our attention. We have to focus on the whole world around us, not just those parts that are pleasant. We are called to care for more than the people we get along with. It is fairly easy to do something for someone whom you know will reciprocate, but often in our lives we are called to serve others who cannot possibly return the favor.

The part of this Gospel that I keep thinking about is the "least ones." I had a hospital call one Saturday when I was at a parish in Dayton, Ohio. It was a sad visit; the couple I came to see just had a still-born baby. They were in so much pain. We talked for a while and the parents wanted me to bless their baby. We prayed and I blessed the child in his mother's arms.

After I left the room, I stopped by the Wendy's there in the hospital. I was dressed in my priest clothes in a Catholic hospital. While I was standing in the long line, up ahead of me was an older man who was dressed in ragged clothes. He looked like he hadn't had a shower in a while. He then looked back at me and yelled, "Hey Father, would you buy me a hamburger and a cup of coffee?" With everyone in line looking at me, what could I say? I paid for his meal and he left, only to be met by security and escorted out of the building.

As I was driving home I thought a lot about that chance encounter. I knew the reason I paid for his meal was because of the people around me. I was not a good follower of Jesus at that moment. But I am thankful for that experience because it brought to my attention that I am called to serve others in unlikely places as well.

We may never know at what moment and in what form Jesus will cross our paths. It could be the person begging on the street. It could be the needy family for whom you are buying food at Christmas. It could be the person you see struggling with their groceries in the store parking lot. Perhaps it's the person in front of you or behind you in church. In our daily lives, Jesus has many faces. Our challenge is to recognize Jesus in everyone, especially one of the "least ones."

I hope you've enjoyed reading my thoughts on Matthew's gospel as much as I enjoyed writing them.

If you live in or are visiting the Cincinnati area, I'd like to invite you to visit us at St. John the Evangelist Catholic Church in West Chester, Ohio. No matter what your present status in the Catholic Church, no matter what your current family or marital situation, no matter what your past or present religious affiliation, no matter your personal history, age, background, race, or color-you are invited, welcomed, accepted, loved, and respected at St. John.

Check out our web site at, www.stjohnwc.org

Made in the USA
Monee, IL
11 August 2023

40807822R00098